or before th

Outside
Belongings

Outside
Belongings

Elspeth Probyn

Routledge
New York & London

Published in 1996 by

Routledge
29 West 35 Street
New York, NY 10001

Published in Great Britain in 1996 by

Routledge
11 New Fetter Lane
London EC4P 4EE

Printed in the United States of America.

Parts of Chapter 2 appear in *Sexy Bodies: The Strange Carnalities of Feminism* (eds. Elizabeth Grosz and Elspeth Probyn, Routledge 1995); Chapter 4 was published in *GLO: A Journal of Lesbian and Gay Studies*, Vol. 2 (1995).

Library of Congress Cataloging-in-Publication Data

Probyn, Elspeth, 1958–
    Outside belongings / by Elspeth Probyn.
    p.   cm.
    Includes bibliographical references.
    ISBN 0-415-91583-X.
    1. Women—Psychology. 2. Gay communities. 3. Feminist theory. I. Title.
HQ1206.P744   1996   95-26496
    305.42—dc20   CIP

contents

acknowledgments   vii

introduction   I
Approximating Belonging

1   17
On the Surface

2   37
Becoming-Horse
Transports in Desire

3   63
"Love in a Cold Climate"
Queer Belongings in Québec

4   93
Suspended Beginnings
Of Childhood and Nostalgia

5   125
Disciplinary Desires
The Outside of Queer
Feminist Cultural Studies

postscript   155

notes   157

bibliography   165

index   177

acknowledgments

My heartfelt thanks to those who read and commented on previous drafts: Marty Allor, Fadi Abou-Rihan, Ann Game, Anna Gibbs, Line Grenier, Larry Grossberg, Judith Halberstam, Lise Harou, Kevin Koppelson, Val Morrison, and Kim Sawchuk. I am particularly indebted to Marty, Larry, and Kim, who came to my rescue at the last hour to read the final version.

I want to thank those who invited me to present parts of this book at conferences as well as the friends who enrich academic wandering: Marie-Luise Angerer, Lauren Berlant, Julia Creet, Moira Gatens, Sue Golding, Liz Grosz, shassan Hage, Melissa Hardie, Val Hartouni, Caren Kaplan, Kate Lilley, George Lipsitz, Robert Martin, Minoo Moellem, Paul Patton, Jules Pidduck, Fitz Pool, Robbie Schwartzwald, Beth Seaton, Sherry Simon, Zoe Sofoulis, and many others. I also want to thank my students at the Université de Montréal, especially Diane Breton, François Gagnon, Fanny Roy-Huard, and my research assistants, Katarina Soukup and Julie Garneau. The members of the Groupe de recherche sur la citoyennété culturelle helped me to consider more closely notions of citizenship. My time at UCSD Women's Studies Program challenged me to rethink Québec in California, and the University of Western Sydney, Nepean, provided a much-needed bridge into Australian academic culture. My love as always to my family, Stephen, Jane, and John Probyn and Nick Dinnage, who, even if they don't always follow, are steadfast in their support.

I gratefully acknowledge the funding that enabled this research: FCAR-Nouveaux chercheurs, FCAR-Subventions aux équipes, and the Social Sciences and Humanities Research Council of Canada.

introduction
Approximating
Belonging

Perhaps because I grew up with a bleak architecture that enclosed its inhabitants and hid them away from distant neighbors, I find the architecture of
Montréal especially intriguing. The working-class and formerly working-
class parts of the city are strung together and defined by a network of
balconies; often these are enhanced by outside staircases that curve their
way up to the second and third floors. In winter, these staircases make
absolutely no sense; covered in snow, they resemble nothing more than icy
water slides. But as soon as the spring sun emerges, balconies become the
places where life is conducted. In David Fennario's terms, the famous
response to the question of where you are going for summer holiday is
"Balconville." And as his play of the same name makes clear, Balconville is
the space of a convergence; for Fennario, it is evidence that in certain spaces
working-class ties and sensibilities can overcome the traditional hard line
of linguistic separation between *les Anglais et les Francos*.

Since the productions of his play in the late '70s and early '80s, there
has been a further loosening of the categorization of all Anglophones as
capitalist swine and all Francophones as the victims of English imperialism.
As Sherry Simon writes,

> "Montréal's human geography for a long time seemed to confirm the most
> elemental verities of economic domination and cultural difference.... But
> as might be expected in our increasingly hybrid present, neither the neat
> geometrical divisions nor the polarizations of identity they suggest seem
> quite as certain today." (1991: 22)

A mixture of factors (both gentrification and the appeal of low rents)
draws a heterogeneous bunch of inhabitants, but Balconville remains.
While other cities feature balcony architecture (though in my experience
not as many as one might think), there is a certain singularity to
Montréal's balconies. In Jean-Claude Marsan's description, the late-19th-
and early-20th-century type of housing typical within Francophone quar-
ters is marked by distinct elements: notably by the habitual front balcony

which served "as a natural extension of the lodging." He speculates that "as the majority of this type of housing was destined for a newly arriving population from the rural world, where galleries and verandas were usual, it may be that this equipment was considered to be necessary" (1994: 270). From balconies early incarnation as outside parlors, people continue to actually live on them: television sets are installed outside, as well as armchairs, sofas, herbs, flowers, or entire vegetable gardens, radios, awnings, and curtains—the whole resembling a tent city, without the veil of canvas, on upper floors above busy city streets.

Living on the outside for the summer entails a proximity to others as well as the drawing of new frontiers. In my own case in the area of Mile-End (a mixed neighborhood of Jews, Greeks, Portuguese, Anglos, Francos), my back balcony (or more precisely, *la galérie*) is a mere foot and a half wide and joins me with my two neighbors, women with whom I often converse. Our moments of conversation are ordered by an inaudible rhythm so that we talk when we talk and at other moments proceed as if we were alone in enwalled gardens: I tune out when one is entertaining her boyfriend; the other leaves me alone when I'm courting with a girl. By chance, it is a building with all women tenants except for one sole male. While we do not live free of the fear that women face on the outside, we have nonetheless reassured ourselves of the relative difficulty of anyone reaching our balconies. Not a stone's throw away, we face the Hasidim *schul* where boys of various sizes play loudly on a worn patch of concrete. As I watch the exchanges of tenderness and discipline between the boys and their rabbi teachers, the spectacle of a woman's body in shorts goes unremarked; indeed, I am rendered invisible until I hear a shout: "Hey lady, throw down the ball," or a snatch of humor from these serious young men: "Hey missus, throw down the cat." To the east, and under the church which looks Greek Orthodox but houses Polish Catholics, a bunch of twentysome-things have created something that looks like a '60s commune on the second-floor roof. We share a taste for the seventies when it comes to music, and ABBA and the Village People stir up the humid night air. In turn, their building abuts on some renovated condos, the inhabitants of which hide behind a trellis.

While this may sound like a romantic picture, what is more striking is the very ordinariness, and indeed the fundamental shabbiness, that renders Montréal "*une jolie laide*" (as the apt if rather sexist expression would have it). It is its *so-what* singularity that begs certain questions. As my neighbor Sherry Simon asks, "Not only do immigrants but also those who are 'from here' share increasingly complex forms of cultural allegiance. How are we going to find an adequate symbolic language to account for the fractured and plural identities of those (more and more numerous) who are committed to Québec and yet participate in several cultures?" (1991: 23).

For me, living in this jumbled quartier and city brings to the fore several preoccupations that have been part of my work over the last several years. The experience of quite literally living on the outside during the summer months (though as I describe in the third chapter, winter brings another type of articulation of bodies and belonging) speaks of something more than the term *identity* can catch, a cohabitation that goes beyond the limited concept of tolerance. Quite simply, this experience inspires a mode of thinking about how people get along, how various forms of belonging are articulated, how individuals conjugate difference into manners of being, and how desires to become are played out in everyday circumstances. It lends an urgency to questions about the materiality of cultural locality and revitalizes that staple of cultural studies inquiry: How do individuals make sense of their lives? For me, it also means another way of going about asking these questions; in very banal ways, I put to work what I think was a compliment when one of my colleagues called me "*une sociologue de la peau*," "a sociologist of the skin."

While I take the conceptual elements for this project from several sources, I want to briefly consider the conceptual reach of the notion of a "sociology of the skin." Basically it comes down to a heightened sensitivity to the sensibilities, to being captured by other manners of being and desires for becoming-other that I call belonging. For instance, I am drawn by examples: I seek to examine examples as interstitial moments in the work of articulation. Here I take articulation in Stuart Hall's sense: the process whereby "the articulation of different, distinct elements...can be rearticulated in different ways because they have no necessary 'belongingness'" (1986: 53). The example of the balconies in Montréal has no necessary meaning, yet it exemplifies for me a certain movement as different and distinct elements are brought together, if only momentarily. Lines of class, gender, sex, generation, ethnicity, and race intermingle as people hang out. The balcony is for me a site where one sees an ongoing inbetweenness. It is a small instance, but it highlights the necessity of getting at the minuteness of movement that occurs in the everyday processes of articulation.

This mode of proceeding by way of one's skin through the minute documenting of so-what events and examples carries some risks and requires further explanation. Without belaboring the skin image, I use it here to foreground a certain theoretical and political commitment and awareness that Hall characterizes as feeling "the pressure on our language, to show its workings, to open itself to accessibility" (1992: 289). For me, this foregrounds an engagement with the tangible, the material, and a devotion to trying to realize the virtual as the actual. To replay Donna Haraway's question, "Why should our bodies end at the skin?" (1985: 96), I also want to ask why skin should end at our individual bodies? For what I am trying to capture in these essays is the sense that belonging expresses a desire for more than what is, a yearning to make skin stretch beyond individual needs and wants. I am then committed to finding and experimenting with different modalities of registering the sensation of that longing. It follows that I risk privileging my own perspective. While I am well aware that I walk a thin line that at any time may disappear into narcissism or endless auto-reflexivity, I maintain that the body that writes is integral to the type of figuring I wish to do. It is a body that is fully part of the outside it experiments with. If the angles from which I look and which I seek to create are unrepresentative, they are nonetheless part of the world as I see it becoming. Feminist, dyke, desiring: the examples that interest me at times point to the banality of violence, but more often they speak of instances where individuals are, consciously or not, caught up in working against racism, gynophobia, and homophobia. From where I write, the world is pretty wonderfully weird and diverse and perverse; it is what encourages me to hope that transversal connections between individuals are an everyday actuality, and that the virtual politics of such engagements can be materialized.

In terms of disciplinary belongings, this is a project that strives to be fully interdisciplinary. This requires an acute attentiveness to writing, to reading, to looking, to being interested. Like the processes of articulation which involve making evident the movement together of different distinct elements, I seek here to mobilize different levels of phenomena: words and things, sounds and sensations, theories and fiction. As an extension of a previous book, *Sexing the Self* (Probyn, 1993), my argument here continues with a certain use of experience, autobiography, and writing. If in that book I laid out a certain theoretical framework to support a nonessential use of the self, here I strive to elaborate a writing practice that is at once theoretical, sociological, experiential, and political. It is a practice focused on intervening in the social, an outside that is the condition of possibility for my writing. I proceed by trying to get within the machinery of what I am describing—to become a part of it. Taking to heart Deleuze's warning against "applying" theory, I attempt to work through and with certain philosophical insights as from within I move forward and out along other surfaces. While this book may be "about" many things, it is propelled by the need to engage an alternative form of theoretical practice that forefronts the perils and joys of writing. And again such writing finds its conditions of possibility in more careful modes of listening, reading, hearing, and seeing. It can therefore never be a question of writing purely for its own sake; as a practice it is completely dependent on how one moves with and within the social.

Here, as elsewhere, I am inspired by the examples of Michel Foucault and Gilles Deleuze. Quite simply, I see life differently because of their writing. And while I know that they are maligned on several fronts, it seems to me that many readings fail to appreciate or even comprehend their sense of humor, of joy, and of the deep urgency of remembering that the art of living or of becoming is a creative endeavor—the only one most of us have. For instance, in his preface to *The Order of Things*, Foucault recalls that his book "first arose out of a passage in Borges, out of the laughter that shattered, as I read the passage, all the familiar landmarks of my thought—*our* thought, the thought that bears the stamp of our age and our geography" (1973: xv). This passage always reminds me of the necessity of a certain sense of wonder so crucial to critical thinking and writing. Borges cites "'a certain Chinese encyclopaedia' in which it is written that 'animals are divided into: (a) belonging to the Emperor, (b) embalmed, (c) tame, (d) sucking pigs, (e) sirens, (f) fabulous, (g) stray dogs, (h) included in the present classification, (i) frenzied, (j) innumerable, (k) drawn with a very fine camelhair brush, (l) *et cetera*, (m) having just broken the water pitcher, (n) that from a long way off look like flies'" (cited in Foucault, 1973: xv).

Foucault goes on to say that his laughter is tinged with unease; this ordering of animals shakes the very ground which we think we order. It participates in "breaking up all the ordered surfaces and all the planes with which we are accustomed to tame the wild profusion of existing things,…to disturb and threaten with collapse our age-old distinction between the Same and the Other" (1973: xv). For Foucault, it is not merely that the encyclopedia indicates an incongruous order; it also presents us with the dimension of the heteroclite: "In such a state, things are 'laid', 'placed', 'arranged' in sites so very different from one and another that it is impossible to find a place of residence for them, to define a *common locus* beneath them all" (1973: xvii–xviii).

While my own project didn't exactly arise out of laughter, it did start from sheer curiosity and an idiosyncratic wish to trace by hand the outside of the city in which I have lived for longer than any other place. Montréal is a place that imposes official limits to belonging, like the sign laws requiring French to be predominant that until recently banned any public appearance of any other language—and yet it is also a place that exerts a strange and sometimes inexplicable attraction. Beyond Montréal, I have had a lifelong fascination with belonging, an interest that already disturbs any "natural," "authentic" belonging. Hanging out in airports and train and bus stations, I wonder about families with their possessions, heading off to make another life. I think of the ever increasing numbers of refugees and the apatriated—their tremendous courage is both humbling and terrifying.

But again, if you have to think about belonging, perhaps you are already outside. Instead of presuming a common locus, I want to consider the ways in which the very longing to belong embarrasses its taken-for-granted nature. More than an implicit play on *outside belonging* as already *beyond* belonging and identity, I want to raise the ways in which outside belonging operates now not as a substantive claim but as a manner of being. Simply put, I want to figure the desire that individuals have to belong, a tenacious and fragile desire that is, I think, increasingly performed in the knowledge of the impossibility of ever really and truly belonging, along with the fear that the stability of belonging and the sanctity of belongings are forever past. While one might chalk this fear up to postmodernism, or more likely to a pessimism wrought out of the economic crises that most have lived through, I think that the desire to belong lives on, placing us on the outside. And in a climate marked by a widespread politics of polarization, it is of the utmost urgency that we take into account this desire to belong, a desire that cannot be categorized as good or bad, left or right—in short, a desire without a fixed political ground but with immense political possibilities.

As a theoretical term and as a lived reality, I pose the term *outside belonging* against certain categorical tendencies and the rush to place differences as absolute. This is notably a *modus operandi* of that ever-growing phenomenon that passes for identity politics, a politics now played with a vengeance by any number of ideologically incompatible groups: from conservatives as they police the frontiers of certain groups ("the teenage mother"), dismantling programs of affirmative action in the name of anti-identity politics, to a "me-too" strain within cultural theory (to use Richard Dyer's phrase [1994]). Increasingly, it seems that even in progressive circles the heart has fallen out of considerations about identity. Identity has become a set of implacable statements that suppress, at times, questions about what identity really is for.

In the face of the fixity of the categorical logic of identity, I seek to instill some of the movement that the wish to belong carries, to consider more closely the movement of and between categories. In the chapters that follow I argue for singularity in order to capture some of the ways in which we continually move inbetween categories of specificity. While I acknowledge the necessity of zones of specificity, rather than placing them in a hierarchical ranking I want to pay attention to how they are lived out as singular. One way to emphasize the production of singular outside belongings is to place them along with the spaces that Foucault calls heterotopic.

Foucault first raises the idea of heterotopia in his discussion of Borges. Against "utopias," which are comforting, fabulous *no places*, "*Heterotopias* are disturbing...because they make it impossible to name this *and* that, because they shatter or tangle common names, because they destroy 'syntax' in advance, and not only the syntax with which we construct sentences but also that less apparent syntax which causes words and things to 'hold together'" (1973: xviii). In keeping with the ways in which the example of the Chinese encyclopedia disturbs the geography of our

Elspeth Probyn

syntax, heterotopias break up the very ground, the *"tabula* that enables thought to operate upon the entities of our world, to put them in order, to divide them into classes, to group them according to names that designate their similarities and differences" (1973: xvii). Again, against a certain logic of identity which proceeds through division and designation, ultimately producing polarization, the concept of heterotopia provides an analytic space in which to consider forms of belonging outside of the divisiveness of categorizing. After all, the spaces in which we seek belonging ("the spaces that claw and knaw at us") "are not a kind of void, inside of which we could place individuals and things" (Foucault, 1986: 23). The sights and sounds of the spaces in which I sometimes belong are integral to the ways in which I live and think belonging, the ways in which space presses upon us and is in turn fashioned by desires.

Heterotopia designates the coexistence of different orders of space, the materiality of different forms of social relations and modes of belonging. As feminist and queer geographers remind us, space is sexed and gendered, and sex and gender are "spaced" (Bell et al. 1994). While elsewhere (1995) I have argued that it is crucial not to collapse the material and historical ways in which sex and gender are distinctly produced, it is also important to understand that these spaces are delineated through coincidence and not through exclusion. They are produced through specificity and lived out in their singularity. As Foucault puts it, we "live inside a set of relations that delineates sites which are irreducible to one another and absolutely not superimposable on one another" (1986: 23).

Historically, heterotopias emerge and change: there have been heterotopias of crisis, reserved places that hold various orders of sexual manifestations—from menstruating women to the space of military service, which allows a society to have its young men sexually experiment outside of home (and on women and men of another nationality or class), to the honeymoon trip, in which "young women's deflowering could take place 'nowhere'" (1986: 25). According to Foucault, this type of heterotopia has given way to heterotopias of deviation, sites "in which individuals whose behavior is deviant to the required mean and norm are placed" (1986: 25). At the heart of his argument is a conceptualization of the production and regulation of social forms and sites of proximity—the proximating of social relations: "Heterotopia juxtaposes in one real place several different spaces, 'several sites that are in themselves incompatible' or foreign to one another" (Foucault, cited in Soja, 1995: 15). As Edward Soja puts it, these are "places where many spaces converge and become entangled" (1995: 15).

Belonging and heterotopia thus foreground the space of movement—the changing configurations of social relations—and the movement across space. It is perhaps not surprising that this book is littered with examples of various forms of locomotion: trains, planes, horses. They are examples which coincide with Foucault's citing of heterotopic spaces—the ship: "a floating piece of space, a place without a place, that exists by itself, that is closed in on itself and at the same time is given over to the infinity of the sea" (1986: 27); the train: "It is something through which one goes, it is also something by means of which one can go from one point to another, and then it is also something that goes by" (1986: 24). These are then examples of the inextricable doubledness of heterotopic spaces: at once inside and outside, they propose that "a thing's place [is] no longer anything but a point in its movement" and that "space takes for us the form of relations among sites" (1986: 23).

One of the central arguments of this book is that the outside (*le dehors*) is a more adequate figure for thinking about social relations and the social than either an interior/exterior or a center/marginal model. The notion of outside supposes that we think in terms of "relations of proximity," or the surface, "a network in which each point is distinct...and has a position in relation to every other point in a space that simultaneously holds and separates them all" (Foucault, 1987: 12). I am well aware of the risks of proposing such figures over those of a more traditional vocabulary. Some may contend that conceiving of the social in terms of the outside and as surface allows for a flattening out of the structural inequalities that continue to do violence, that as terms they erase acknowledgment of oppression, that they evacuate interiority, etc. While these objections may be motivated by a justified concern that a political agenda is being jettisoned in favor of superficiality, I think that there is some confusion here. For instance, Hayden White argues that "there is no center to Foucault's discourse. It is all surface—and intended to be so...Foucault's discourse is wilfully superficial" (cited in Halperin, 1995: 211). In turn, White seems to conflate several separate points. To be sure, the question of the surface and style are intimately connected, if we understand style to be a manner of writing that is inseparable from the object of, and the political motivation for, writing. Perhaps the problem in part is that surface is taken as if it were an object rather than a process. This is why I prefer to think in terms of *rendering surface* or *surfacing*, the processes by which things become visible and are produced as the outside. And even without any appreciation of Foucault's historical analyses of how the visible is produced, it seems merely stubborn to insist that there is no relation between the outside and the inside and the forces that produce at any moment something that we call the surface. As I attempt to show, the surface is not to be posed as ineluctable but rather as a way of configuring the lines of force that compose the social, lines of force that are by their very nature *deeply* material and historical.

In a different vein, Biddy Martin argues that attention to the surface and the outside denies the affectivity of interiority. Given Martin's early and productive reading of Foucault (1982), it is intriguing that her argument against the surface should bypass Foucault's sense of surface. In reference to current American queer theory, she argues that "surfaces...take priority over interiors and depths and even rule conventional approaches to them out of bounds as inevitably disciplinary and constraining" (1994: 106). However, rather than ruling out the positivity of the surface as a conceptual figuring of the social, her comments speak more to a certain "insiderist" trend in cultural criticism. Of more concern is her claim that,

> too thorough an evacuation of interiority, too total a collapse of the boundaries between public and private, and too exclusive an understanding of psychic life as the effect of normalization can impoverish the language we have available for thinking about selves and relationships, even as they apparently enrich our vocabularies for thinking about social construction. (1994: 106)

While again the ground of Martin's critique is American queer studies, the opposition of interiority on the one hand and social construction on the other is somewhat misleading. In contrast, I want to focus on the ways in which the surface presupposes a rendering visible of the forces which constitute the outside and the inside as dichotomous. I wish to emphasize the ways in which belonging is situated as threshold: both public and private, personal and common, this entails a very powerful mode of subjectification. It designates a profoundly affective manner of being, always performed with the experience of being within and inbetween sets of social relations. It precisely emphasizes and moves with that experience. Moreover, belonging cannot be an isolated and individual affair. Conceptualizing social relations and subjectification in terms of the outside renews an awareness of their very relationality.

Perhaps most importantly, the longing in belonging on the outside forces us to think about the role of desire in a fully social sense. Here I am particularly inspired by Deleuze's use of desire and by Elizabeth Grosz's work on figuring lesbian desire (1994b).[1] Briefly put, desire is productive; it is what oils the lines of the social; it produces the pleats and the folds which constitute the social surface we live. It is through and with desire that we figure relations of proximity to others and other forms of sociality. It is what remakes the social as a dynamic proposition, for if we live within a grid or network of different points, we live through the desire to make them connect differently. To bring what seems to be far away up close remains for me the object of writing. The desire to belong propels, even as it rearranges, the relations into which it intervenes. Desire touches off and sets into motion different possibilities, a movement of attraction that Foucault sees in "a woman's gesture in a window, a door left ajar, the smile of a guard before a forbidden threshold" (1987: 28).

It will become obvious that in these essays I am concerned with the singularity of lesbian desire. By this I do not mean that we can pose one essential, authentic lesbian desire; rather, I wish to articulate desire as that which gives life to static categories that would underpin claims to inclusive essentialism. Put in other terms, singularity is what emerges after we have enumerated our differences—moments and movements that establish contact across a geography of division. In the course of these essays, I also grapple with different uses of the term *queer*. Written as they were across the moment of queer theory's full emergence, these pieces are at times caught up in the euphoria of queer's possibilities; at times I move away from ideas I consider to be restricting. In one of the clearest expositions of queer theory's positivity and constraints, Judith Butler argues that "if the term 'queer' is to be a site of collective contestation, the point of departure for a set of historical reflections and futural imaginings, it will have to remain that which is, in the present, never fully owned, but always and only redeployed, twisted, queered from a prior usage and in the direction of urgent and expanding political purposes" (1993: 228). She cautions as well that "as expansive as the term 'queer' is meant to be, it is used in ways that enforce a set of overlapping divisions" (1993: 228).

Whereas Butler sets out the "temporality of the term" (1993: 223), I wish to consider its spatiality: both where queer plays out and ways to make it an active proposition so that it re-creates experimental space. Along with Eve Kosofsky Sedgwick, I want to consider queer as movement, to turn queer into a verb (a sense already evident in Butler's proposition that the noun *queer* itself is twisted and queered). As Sedgwick notes, "The word 'queer' itself means *across*—it comes from the Indo-European root—*twerkw*, which also yields the German *quer*, Latin *torquere* (to twist), English *athwart*" (1993: xii). If, in Sedgwick's formulation, queer is an "immemorial current...relational, and strange," this idea plays out for me in the desire to work along what she calls "the fractal intricacies of language, skin, migration, state" (1993: xii, 9).

It is in this way that desire, outside belonging, and writing are about the modes of effecting movement, movement aimed at creating a momentum for change in social relations, a way of enacting "relationships of effectuation" (Gordon, 1981), "relationships of differentiation, of creation, of innovation" (Foucault, 1984: 28). What I trace here is the positivity of desire as it produces new relations and relationships among individuals, things, groups, etc.—a current that short-circuits the categorial order of things. It should be clear that working within positivity does not necessarily result in a celebratory rhetoric; rather, desire as social force compels us to think beyond the terminal points of either celebration or *ressentiment*. I write in order to remind myself of the ways in which belonging hinges on not belonging, to raise the ways in which the manners of being at the threshold may provide another perspective from which to view the complexities of identity, difference, subjectivity, and desire. My aim here is to draw up a certain "general topology of thinking, which always start[s] with the 'neighboring' of singularities...a carnal and vital topography" (Deleuze, 1986: 126).

Before moving on, I wish to simply and, I hope, clearly set out some of the epistemological and political stakes of the mode of theorizing that I endeavor to embody. I start from the recognition that we are in the midst of becoming-other, a statement that is hardly startling. I follow with the fairly obvious observation that one possible role among many for those of us who write and think about the social is to get as close as possible to the mutations of movements, to catch ourselves within the transversality of our times. To do this adequately and with as much *justesse* as possible, I engage a certain style, a mode of getting about, that comprehends as it surpasses the ordinary sense of aesthetics.

As those familiar with Foucault will know, style and aesthetics combine in a project aimed at diagnosing actuality at the same time that "lines of actualization require another mode of expression" (Deleuze, 1989: 192). As part of a diagnostic of the becoming-other of ourselves and of the social that we inhabit, I find it necessary to proceed along the skin—skin which is both surface and redolent of certain orders and ordering of sociality. It is scented with possibilities: the virtual becoming actual before one's eyes, ears, hands. Proceeding through examples, fragments, bits and pieces, I take up anything and everything I can in the hope of rendering a multitude of specificities into a glimpse of singularity. This is, as Deleuze puts it, to go "from one specific place to another, from one singular point to another...producing thus effects of transversality and no longer universality, functioning as a privileged point of exchange or crossing" (1986: 97).

My own project is but one point of exchange, one example of multiple criss-crossing, but I hope that my observations come to the surface, leaving traces on the outside that may encourage other movements, hopes of becoming, and alternative belongings.

1

On the
Surface

Start with a proposition: instead of inquiring into the depths of sociality, let us consider the social world as surface. Follow with questions: What to do with all the various longings for belonging? What to do with the range of desiring identities that are displayed all around? Here I slide from "identity" to "belonging," in part because I think that the latter term captures more accurately the desire for some sort of attachment, be it to other people, places, or modes of being, and the ways in which individuals and groups are caught within wanting to belong, wanting to become, a process that is fueled by yearning rather than the positing of identity as a stable state. This movement of desiring belonging is for me a defining feature of our postmodern, postcolonial times, part of the contemporary "perplexity of living," to use Walter Benjamin's phrase. Benjamin's phrase is, in turn, taken up by Homi Bhabha in his argument about the conditions of "dissemination." If the "perplexity of living" captures for Bhabha the complexity of the postcolonial situation, it also recalls for me something of the queerness of all forms of living, the very *umheimlich*-ness of social life. This is not to collapse the notions of queer and postcolonial but to consider belonging, at this historical conjuncture, as queer. Keeping these historical processes distinct, I want to learn from different manners of becoming and of belonging. Benjamin's phrase inspires me to study the inbetweenness of belonging, of belonging not in some deep authentic way but belonging in constant movement, modes of belonging as surface shifts. In this chapter, I argue that it is necessary, at this time, to insist on the surface nature of belonging. I use Benjamin's phrase as a way of immediately foregrounding some of the stakes in proposing this shift to the surface, of returning a sense of perplexity to the study of desiring identities and of longings to become. If I want to reinvigorate the idea that living is bewildering, strange, and sometimes wonderful, I also want to emphasize the magic of ordinary desires and return a feeling for that magic to cultural studies. This is a call neither for a naive attitude of celebration nor a stance of innocence before the brutalities of contemporary life. It does, however, depend on a sharpened acuity to the machinations and configurations of desires as they play out on the surface—a surface upon which all manner of desires to belong are conducted in relations of proximity to each other; a milieu in which different modes of belonging fold and twist the social fabric of life, so that we find ourselves in unexpected ways using desires for belonging as threads that lead us into unforeseen places and connections. In the course of these essays, I attempt to render somehow more evident, somehow more tangible, somehow more singular the very so-what expressions of cultural belonging in which I move. I start from my own experience of being caught up in movements of belonging, and like the scribe poring over texts she traces as she illuminates them, I wish to walk within what Edward Said calls "worldliness," where "sensuous particularity as well as historical continency...exist at the same level of surface particularity as the textual object itself" (cited in Bhabha, 1994: 140).

Particularity and sensuality, surfaces and the outside, images that hit and move one to return to the minuteness of the social surface, the refusal to generalize—these are key themes, the theoretical underpinnings of which I will endeavor to explicate. They also direct me to thinking about ways of telling, modes of being in the world, and technologies of writing. Thus, before I turn to the theoretical problematics that move this book, I want to briefly cite a tale of magic, a story that catches at one way of seeing the interrelation of history, place, and sexuality, one mode of performing the translation of lesbian desires across continents, ages, and forms of knowledge.

In her novel, *The Dyke and the Dybbuk* (1993), Ellen Galford takes up the figure of the dybbuk. While the tale is firmly situated within the tenets of Jewish mythology that give rise to this spirit-figure, the mission of Galford's dybbuk is to abet the vengeance against a certain Gittel by Anya, who is, in her own words, "neither one thing nor the other.... Not quite Jew...not quite Gentile." Her fury at Gittel does not quite efface the memory of their times together: "Not quite a woman—because I wanted to do things with Gittel that only a man was supposed to do; not quite a man—because I wanted Gittel to do the same things back to me" (223). Kokos, the dybbuk, is materialized by a curse that Anya has put upon Gittel for having dropped her for a good Torah scholar. It is, says Kokos, a masterpiece of a curse, "a verbal edifice of Byzantine intricacy" with "passages burrowing into the distant future" (6). The gist of the curse is that Gittel "should disappoint her husband by bearing only daughters; and that the surviving first-borns of the female line should be similarly afflicted unto the thirty-third generation" (7). The line of the curse then stretches across centuries of migrating female first-borns, only to gather itself in London, where love and history play out in the final female first-born falling in love with the original curse-spinner (Anya, now translated into a savvy butch cab driver).

It is a splendid tale and one that through a singular dyke sensibility tells of the experience of being "between two lines." While retaining its own singularity—among other things, written within the codes of lesbian romance—it nonetheless replays within the register of fiction what Bhabha calls

> the experience of migration…[which] in the nation of others, becomes a time of gathering…gatherings in the ghettos or cafés of city centers; in the uncanny fluency of another's language; gathering the signs of approval and acceptance, degrees, discourses, disciplines; gathering the memories of underdevelopment, of other worlds lived retroactively; gathering the past in a ritual of revival; gathering the present. (1994: 139)

While my project has different inflections from Bhabha's, and certainly is of a different order than Galford's, it endeavors to move in the same manner. Thus, while Bhabha's attention is to "the supplementary narrative of nationness that 'adds' to without 'adding up'" (1994: 160), in tracing out the surface of sexual/national/sexual belonging I seek to enumerate singularities in such a way that they may overpower any generalization, any simple adding up to a general statement of identity. As Bhabha states, the point of cultural criticism is to "keep open a supplementary space for the articulation of cultural knowledges that are adjacent and adjunct but not necessarily accumulative": "The 'difference' of cultural knowledge that 'adds to' but does not 'add up' is the enemy of the *implicit* generalization of knowledge or the implicit homogenization of experience " (1994: 163).

In a quite different project, though one that is complementary to Bhabha's, the Italian philosopher Giorgio Agamben lays out very abstract and elegant terms for an alternative conception of relations of sociality, terms that refuse the doubled lines of essence or generality. Key to his conceptualization of "the coming community" is the notion of "la singularité quelconque" (1990). Michael Hardt translates *quelconque* as "whatever" and notes that, "as Agamben makes clear...'whatever' (*qualunque* or *quelconque*) refers to precisely that which is neither particular nor general, neither individual nor generic" (1993: I). *Quelconque* can also be translated as "so-what," and I like both senses of the term. For if "whatever" fits easily within a queer lexicon, *quelconque* as "so-what" catches up with a dreaded question, that potential response to all cultural critique: "So what?"

Against a certain line within cultural studies which aggrandizes the ordinary, romanticizes the banal, and turns us all into popular heros, the interjection of "so what?" is deeply humbling. At the same time, the phrase *so what* serves as an injunction to think belonging and relations of sociality in their very singularity—to think belonging in terms of manners of being, yet again a being that refers not to an ontological ordering of essences but to the very conjuncture that brings forth its manners. Or, as Agamben argues, "The Whatever here relates to singularity not in its indifference with respect to a common property (to a concept, for example: being red, being French, being Muslim), but only in its being *such as it is*" (1993: 1). Being is thus divorced from an inscription of generic properties. Agamben charts a way of thinking belonging that insists on the ontological experience of being within relations of belonging even as it refuses an ontology of belonging based in the individual possession of an intrinsic quality.

To continue in the vein of initial clarifications, the relation of singularity to specificity needs to be posed. While singularity is not a new concept, Agamben makes it the central tenet of his book, all the while refusing to specify the distinction between specificity and singularity. Thus, left on my own to confuse matters, I understand "specificity" to refer to zones of possible forms of belonging: being lesbian, being Welsh, being woman, being red, etc. To use yet other terms, the movement from specificity to singularity can be understood as processes that render the virtual actual—the ways in which the general becomes realized by individuals as singular. Simply put, we do not live our lives as general categories: as a lesbian I should do this; as a feminist I ought to do that. While there have been times when the imperatives of the category meant that individuals became subsumed under the rules of the identity category to which they wished to belong, it seems now that the specificities of those identities may offer alternative modes of individuation that spill over the boundaries of the category.

Specificity can be understood as the necessary zones of difference, but these zones, be they of race, class, sexuality, or gender, are the points from where we depart in order to live out our singular lives. Of course, the specificities of difference are crucial, but they must not be allowed to translate into an ensemble of exhortations that constrict—for instance, when identity becomes a set of hard and fast rules that police comportment. Of course, I am saying nothing new, especially to those who have been the object of such scrutiny. For instance, my understanding of the world has benefited greatly from the courageous writing of lesbians of color whose work forms the ground of any current thinking about the strange and sometimes strained articulations one has to perform between and among categories of difference—women like Jewelle Gomez, who write of the processes by which they have arrived at forming "a tenuous yet definite community" with others; women who speak of their relation to femaleness, to community, of their attachment to other women, to families, of different "relationships to the ideas of maleness, femaleness, and Blackness" (Gomez, 1995: 135–136).

In a small way, I also hope to encourage the movement away from thinking and living difference and specificity as negative: to continue with others the task of conceiving specificity as the ground from where we move into the positivity of singularity. Working from desiring identities and belongings then foregrounds the way in which we are propelled into forms of living with ourselves and with others. This is to turn identity inside out so that instead of capturing us under its regime of difference as a negative measure, the desire of belonging becomes a force that proffers new modes of individuation and of being. Zones of specificity and difference, at different times and under certain circumstances, then may be yielded and lived out as singular.

To further muddy the theoretical waters, I understand singularity in much the same way that Foucault uses "necessity." M. Hannah helpfully characterizes a major aspect of Foucault's method—"his descriptive pursuit of the vanishing point where the very 'surface' of things (for example, discursive events), their otherwise mute, preinterpreted existence, bespeaks their necessity, where possibility imperceptibly disappears into actuality" (1993: 358). Singularity is thus *rendered*, not posited; it is to be produced in the processes of reducing possibility (as with a sauce or stock). In Hannah's vivid image, "It is best to think of possibility as disappearing not through the amputation of large chunks accounted for by monolithic causal forces, but instead through a complex, uneven erosion, like the cleaning of skeletons by flesh beetles" (358). To be more prosaic, the process of singularizing forms of belonging passes through the minute description of the specificity of things, the "adding to" directed not at "adding up" to some totality but at a description of "exclusive actuality": what emerges from what is said now, here, and nowhere else (Foucault, 1972: 27–28).[1]

It should be clear that singularity cannot be understood as a voluntary performance, an individualized state of affairs whereby we happily proclaim or exchange identities like changes of clothes. The movement between specificity and singularity is a process that is at times hard trodden, at others even impossible. Again, my use of belonging wishes precisely to capture the ways in which individuals may wish to belong, knowing full well that belonging is not an individual action, that it is always conducted within limits. Just as difference is more often than not first realized when it is described in a thrown epithet, we negotiate our desires for belonging as through a maze of club rules (including Marx's rule about not wanting to belong to any club that would have him). What I want to get at are the ways in which the range of specificities that we may inhabit comes together in singularity.

As Agamben argues, singularity is rendered within and out of the material constraints and historical limits of "being-said," the limits of difference as a personal possession:

> In this conception, such-and-such being is reclaimed from its having this or that property, which identifies it as belonging to this or that set, to this or that class (the reds, the French, the Muslims)—and it is reclaimed not for another class nor for the simple generic absence of any belonging, but for its being-*such*, for belonging itself. (1993: 1–2)

Agamben posits that if belonging is not defined by any property, its possibility is always circumscribed by limits, the limits of "being-called": "not

being-red, but being-*called*-red" (1993: 10). Obviously, attention to the performative and the perlocutionary nature of language is now a common
theme (for example, in the work of Judith Butler or Eve Sedgwick). And
less recently, the role of language in the attribution of difference was one
of the key points that Stuart Hall took from Althusser when, at the end of
his essay "Signification, Representation, Ideology" (1985), he raised the
example of teaching his son that he was black and not brown. If not a novel
point, it bears repeating that the terrain of difference is deeply inscribed by
the historical limits imposed by "being-called." These limits then constitute a condition of possibility for belonging as well as the conditions for
calling into question the inscription of difference: "Being-called—the
property that establishes all possible belongings (being-called-Italian, -dog,
-Communist)—is also what can bring them all back radically into question" (Agamben, 1993: 10).

I admit that when I first read Agamben's book *La communauté qui vient:
Une théorie de la singularité quelconque*, I was attracted by the spareness and the
abstraction of his propositions. However, I will also avow that while I found
him appealing, there was a certain crypticality and unintelligibility to his
énoncés. Nonetheless, or maybe because of this, I was struck by his articulation of belonging as fundamentally impersonal but crucial. For, at the
time, as now, I was trying to figure modalities which could radically deper-
sonalize identity yet not do away with those desires for belonging, those
desiring identities I saw all around me: on the street, at queer conferences,
in feminist journals, etc. For those familiar with Agamben's work, it will
be clear that I deform him just as I am inspired by his work. I make no apol-
ogy for this; in fact, it is inevitable that given the pressures that inform my
own thinking (most notably of feminist and lesbian and gay critical theories and practices), I should do so. Most significantly, I inject desire, and
moreover lesbian or queer desire, into considerations of belonging. While it
is desire understood not as an individual possession but rather as a relational force among individuals, desire remains for me crucial in thinking
about belonging. And, as will become evident, I read Agamben alongside
Deleuze, whom in turn I read with Foucault.

All this said, it was reading Agamben, now a few years ago, that set
me off, or rather accompanied me as I considered the weird and queer
turns that belonging takes in Montréal. Because of its bilingual and many-

cultured materiality, Montréal embodies a constant inbetweenness. This inbetweenness can be perceived in any number of ways: from the constant way that one is always in between two languages, cultures, and histories (even as it "officially" has only one language, and hence culture) to the ways in which Montréal is posed as apart from the rest of Québec (for instance, when it comes to "tolerance" toward gays, lesbians, feminists, immigrants, etc.) at the same time that it functions metonymically for the whole of Québec. It is a space that contains a multitude of "being-calleds": a place of incessant attempts to linguistically name, a culture spun within the slippages of translation.

As I thought about the singularities of belonging within Montréal, it also happened to be winter, a season that in this climate always raises the question of why anyone in their right mind would want to be here, let alone profess belonging. But it was not quite by chance that the rigors of winter turned my mind to questioning forms of belonging, for if, as Bhabha says, to speak of the English weather is "to invoke, at once, the most changeable and immanent signs of national difference" (1994: 169), then to live the Montréal winter is to be faced with a welter of minute signs signifying the parameters of belonging. From remarks like "You must find it hard here in the winter," spoken by those who have always lived here, who truly belong, to the sight of saris trailing in the snow, to brash young Québécois dudes wearing thin leather jackets open to the waist as they fight the winds howling down Rue Ste. Catherine, winter here is an ensemble of seemingly immanent signs of difference. But this is not to consider winter as having some deep meaning: it has little intrinsic quality, it is performed at a level of so-whatness. Winter is something that is difficult to conceive of as a desired property, although surviving it is necessary. It does, however, call forth manners of being-such that are performed in the hardness of a winter cityscape: a city in winter semiotically pitted against the pure whiteness of the country; a dirty, slutty, slushy city where the non-indigenous stand out; a place that we have nonetheless come to in the hopes of something or other—of happiness, of change, of merely getting by. A place of mixed longings, the mythic point of arrival for young gays and lesbians driven from the isolation of the outer regions, it is, as Bhabha puts it, "to the city that the migrants, the minorities, the diasporic come to change the history of the nation" (1994: 169–170). Drawn to the tolerance of specificities that supposedly thrives in the city, individuals then come to live it in singular ways.

But the singularity remains unpossessable. Weighed down by the innumerable layers of protection against the weather, silenced in the minus-40-something cold, there is utterly no reason why anyone should want at this moment to belong. This scene returns me to the way in which Agamben undercuts any transcendental quality that might rise above belonging, that might place belonging on a transcendental level. Explicating the Latin phrase for "whatever," he notes that "*quodlibet ens* is not 'being, it does not matter which', but rather 'being such that it always matters'. The Latin always already contains, that is, a reference to the will (*libet*). Whatever being has an original relation to desire" (1993: 1). Here the common sense of "whatever" as being anything and everything, as no matter which, as being inconsequential, on the sidelines, etc., is turned inside out. For me, if not for Agamben, it is the very forcefulness of desire, desire as force, that can turn the anything and everything into a question of the singularity of the desire to make the "no matter which" *matter*. Those placed on the sidelines, as inconsequential, then disrupt the sequencing of the dominant order, shift the view of the center by living the periphery in the metropole.

While Agamben does not name the "whatever" as such, the terms of his thinking closely describe the position, the manners, of being postcolonial. Indeed, the "coming community" could be seen as the becoming postcolonial of the West. This is, of course, not to lose the singularity of the "meaning of home and belonging" for those who have come "across the 'middle passage,' or the central European steppes, across those distances, and cultural difference" that Bhabha defines within the experience of migration (1994: 139). And whereas for Bhabha it is a question of the postcolonial and women, and not explicitly of the queer, I take the risk of articulating queer and postcolonial. It is, of course, a considerable risk that could do great damage to the distinct specificities of conditions of possibility of different forms of belonging. However, it is also undeniable that in countless cultural expressions of the colony and the postcolony, from Lawrence to Mitford, the colonial is queerly sexed. As Sabina Sawhney argues of Lawrence's India, the entire continent is figured in terms of an object of desire to be seduced by England (Sawhney, 1995: 205). In Nancy

Mitford's novel *Love in a Cold Climate*, it comes as no surprise that Cedric Hampton, the heir to the Montdore estate, is both Canadian and queer. Even worse, he hails from Nova Scotia, described as "a transatlantic Isle of Wight.... 'No thanks'." As the narrator puts it, 'It was our idea to live in capital cities and go to the Opera alight with diamonds, 'Who is that lovely woman?' and Nova Scotia was clearly not a suitable venue for such doings" (1949: 179). It was beyond the pale, indeed the unthinkable, for the lady of the house: "She had never felt interest or curiosity towards those unsuitable people in Canada, they were one of the unpleasant things of life and she preferred to ignore them" (179). In due course, Cedric's queerness overcomes his unfortunate colonialism, and he and Lady Montdore become bosom pals: "I found Cedric, in a pale mauve silk dressing gown, sitting on her bed. They were both rubbing cream into their faces out of a large pink pot. It smelt delicious, and certainly belonged to him" (194). In this case, one can say that both the colonial and his lady are queered.

Without generalizing from this one instance, *Love in a Cold Climate* is nonetheless a telling instance of the ways in which a postcolonial queer "marginalizes and 'singularizes' the totality of national culture" (Bhabha, 1994: 168). Cedric plays to the hilt within what Bhabha calls "the anterior space of signification" (167); he brings forth and to the surface that most loudly known of secrets—the queer sexuality of the English upper classes—from its place within the guarded confines of institutionalized homosociality (running from cradle to coffin through prep and public schools, the army, and the officers' club). Mitford adroitly condenses the ignorance and the disdain of the English for their colonies with the flaunting of queerness in the figure of Cedric. What cannot be openly admitted (the banality of homosexual practices amongst the English ruling classes) is then clearly proclaimed upon the body of the relocated postcolonial, the postcolonial turned to the manor. Again, this is not to conflate the conditions of possibility of the queer and the postcolonial. It is, rather, to recognize that they are both historical conditions of manners of being, of "being such that it always matters," played out within the dominant order, an order that is slowly mis-recognizing itself. Hence, the belonging that I remark is that which refuses the essential purity of the margin and "insinuating itself into the terms of reference of the dominant discourse...antagonizes the implicit power to generalize, to produce sociological solidity" (Bhabha, 1994: 155).

If this being-such can be seen in the manners of the postcolonial and the queer, it is only inasmuch as we refuse the discourse of identity that seeks to allocate belonging through a certain articulation of difference— the type of discourse whereby difference is tolerated by the dominant order as long as it is encountered only in ethnic restaurants, incarnated in hair- dressers but not sons; difference taught in its own separate class but not across the curriculum; difference eulogized in the liberal strains of "being, it does not matter which"..."Some of my best friends are _____." Against this continuing use of difference, we need to mobilize the exigency of singular difference, to unapologetically encourage its positivity: belong- ing heard not in the pleas for recognition uttered from the sidelines but desire enunciated in such a way as to fundamentally rearrange the place- ment of power, centers and peripheries. The mode of being here is carried in the will and the force of desire to produce belonging as surface, to turn the logics of designation inside out. In cutting the lines of equivalence inherent to dominant notions of identity, of equations of belonging posed in terms of inherent right, we can perhaps render incomprehensible the phrase "go back to where you belong."

One way to reply to such statements is to take them at their surface, their face value, to retort that I do belong here, to shout, "We're queer, we're here, get used to it." A more elaborated strategy must also entail a refusal on the part of the postcolonial and the queer to respond; it must play on retort, on the twisting back of the order of the statement rather than the well-mannered reply to its terms—not the response which is enunciated within the dominant terms, not in resistance with its connota- tions of margin and marginalization, but the retort which takes on author- ity as it folds the terms upon themselves. Or, as Achille Mbembe argues, instead of a logic of resistance "the emphasis should be on the logics of con- viviality, on the dynamics of domesticity and familiarity, which inscribe the dominant and the dominated in the same epistemological field" (1992: 14). The focus here is trained on the relations of proximity between the two, a closeness that upsets the protected space of the dominant—the lady of the Empire and her queer postcolonial heir sharing his pot of face cream.

While Mbembe's argument focuses on the singularities of the post- colonial in Cameroon (and therefore cannot be generalized), drawing on Foucault's concept of governmentality, he also details a conception of postcolonial power that may help to clarify other situations. Central to his argument is the "banality of power" within the postcolony—the ways in which "the champions of state power invent entire constellations of ideas; they select a distinct set of cultural repertoires and powerfully evocative concepts" (1992: 4). The subjects within the postcolony retort these images, turning the "*commandement*" against itself in a baroque display of "the obscene, vulgar and the grotesque" (1992: 1). If, for Mbembe, "the notion of the 'postcolony' simply refers to the specific identity of a given historical trajectory: that of societies recently emerging from the experience of colonization," then "to account for postcolonial relations is thus to pay attention to the workings of power in its minute details, and to the principles of assemblage which give rise to its efficacy" (1992: 2, 4).

Mbembe's argument points precisely to the ways in which the play of power is on the surface, as can be seen "in all the minor circumstances of daily life, such as social networks…culinary practices, leisure activities, modes of consumption, dress styles, rhetorical devices, and the political economy of the body" (1992: 23). A world away, but on a similar wavelength, a postcolonial regime of knowledge plays out in my own banal spot in any number of ways: in *flâning* and sitting in cafés as a national pastime; in the spectacular consumption of nicotine, alcohol, and drugs under the eye of a prudish federal gaze; in the seductive walk of some of the best-dressed women in North America; and so forth.[2] This is certainly not subjection to power in the sense of an *assujettissement* located in the internal recesses of the colonized psyche. It is power producing—desire producing modes of subjectification flaunted at the level of the body: an intimate relation producing the social as outside, as a plurality of surfaces. From a different context, we can also learn from what Tomas Ybarra-Frausto calls the hybrid chicano aesthetic of "*rasquachismo*…a sensibility attuned to mixtures and confluence…a delight in texture and sensuous surfaces" (cited in Bhabha, 1994: 7). Or yet again, in a different situation, Guillermo Gomez-Peña tells of the California/Mexico meeting point as he speaks "from the crevasse, desde aca, desde el medio. The border is the juncture, not the edge…" (1993: 44). Without flattening the important distinctions that exist in such local modes of representation, it is nonetheless instructive to consider what they propose: the position of the juncture as an inbetween state, the moment of articulation whereby, in Gomez-Peña's case, Tijuana remains distinct from San Ysidro even as they are hyphenated, a border culture criss-crossed by bodies, a surface seen from the patrolling helicopters. In the different tones of Ybarra-Frausto, confluence becomes tangible, the flowing movement of surfaces.

As Ybarra-Frausto and Gomez-Peña make explicit, representing, or what I would prefer to call the rendering surface of the conditions of the postcolony requires other modes of writing: the confluence of cultural forms themselves put to service in the task of tracing the surfaces of every-day lives. It is, of course, a mode used by many postcolonial writers: in the mixture of theater, prose, and theory of Gomez-Peña and Coco Fusco; in the translation of theory and poetry that is the writing of Anzaldùa; in Issac Julien's beautiful film essays; in Joan Nestle's or Dorothy Allison's or Mab Segrest's Southern lesbian postcolonial stories, histories, and History. The list could be long, but enumeration is not my intent. And while these examples and others are illuminating, they tend to move from a different point of departure, projects that proceed within specific conditions and yield their own singularity. Inspired by such work, I cannot be satisfied by repeating or citing it as evidence; I must also try to explicate my own process of rendering surface the commingling of forms (of sociality, of examples, of thinking). Thus, from within theory I wish to clarify the status of the surface and the necessary connections to a theory of singularity and the question of the outside.

I do so by returning to Foucault, but this time to a little book that he steadfastly referred to as not belonging to his oeuvre: "Nobody paid any attention to this book, and I'm very glad. It is my secret house, a love affair that lasted a few summers" (cited in Machery, 1992: II). The object of love was the writer Raymond Roussel, and the book was *Raymond Roussel* (1963/1992), which in an interview he called "the archaeology of a passion" (Foucault: 1985). It is a curious thing: Foucault bent over, following the minuteness of Roussel as one might trace by finger the curves of a map in relief, as one might learn by finger the quirks of a lover's body. Foucault says of Roussel's work that it "turns on a singular experience (I mean to say that it has to be put in the singular): the connection of language with this inexistent space which, below the surface of things, separates the interior of their visible face and the periphery of their invisible kernel" (1992: 155).

By all accounts, Roussel was decidedly queer, apparently homosexual and very quirky. It is, of course, not Roussel's homosexuality *per se* that draws Foucault. Roussel's sexuality is only of interest inasmuch as "the private life of an individual, his sexual choices and oeuvre are interlinked, not because the oeuvre translates the sexual life, but because it comprehends both the life and the text" (1985: 104). Roussel is compelling on several levels. The most evident is his attention to *la chosalité*, the thingness of things, the meticulous way in which he focused on images, image-as-image, as surface and not as the expression of a signifier: "the privilege of these images.... A discourse absolutely without depth that runs on the surface of things" (Foucault, 1992: 144). While Foucault speaks of Roussel in passionate tones, it is rapture before the example of the solidly so-what nature of the work, the matter-of-fact *meticulosity* of the details that "add to" but do not "add up."

Roussel is perhaps at his most compelling in his posthumously published book, *Comment j'ai écrit certains de mes livres* (1963) (*How I wrote some of my books*), a bizarre tract wherein he explains his procedure (*le procédé*) by which a phrase, taken by chance, forms and performs a whole story. As Pierre Machery explains, the procedure "consists in a direct intervention on the signifying materiality of words which proceed and direct their fictional economy" (1992: xxiii). In Roussel's own words, "I chose two words nearly identical...for example *billard* (billiards) and *pillard* (a plunderer). Then I added to them similar words but taken in two different senses, and thus I obtained two sentences nearly identical" (1963: 11). In this case, *billard* and *pillard* form the genesis of Roussel's book *Impressions d'Afrique*, the story of a white explorer who writes a book about a black king and plunderer.

Now, for the contemporary reader there are obstacles to appreciating Roussel's work. For a start, the stories carry the sort of generic racism of Roussel's time. I also find his books rather unreadable (one of those uncomfortable situations where the idea outweighs the interest). Roussel is, in Hollywood-speak, "high concept." Sadly enough, he lived with this knowledge, and apart from being briefly taken up by the Surrealists, he lived in the vain hope of being understood and of finding glory through his writing. In Foucault's estimation, and citing Roussel, it wasn't a case of "an exasperated desire for celebrity, but a physical statement: 'What I wrote was encircled by radiance. Every line was repeated to thousands of copies and I wrote with thousands of quills that blazed'" (Foucault, 1992: 199). His last book was written "in the hope that I might have a little posthumous renown for my books" (Roussel, 1963: 35). A compelling image of (and for) a writer, his enormous dedication and the way that he crawled inside ordinary, found phrases in order to make them tell fantastic stories is fascinating, humbling, and slightly ridiculous. For his part, Foucault simply said, "I wrote on Roussel precisely because he was all alone, somewhat abandoned and sleeping on a shelf at José Corti's [the bookseller]" (1985: 104–105). Despite Foucault's denial that *Raymond Roussel* had anything to do with the rest of his work, Roussel appears as exemplary of a major foucauldian theme: here the necessity of "*penser autrement*" meets up with a writer who becomes an anonymous element within the technology of writing, who forces the internal cohesion of language to appear on the surface of the text. This "obscure desire that entertains anyone who writes…one writes to become other than oneself" then meets up with the fact that it is the "modification of one's mode of being that one aims for in the act of writing" (Foucault, 1985: 104).

Beyond the question of Roussel's readability, it is the underlying concept turned surface, a method scrupulously involved in making "language yield towards things," that fascinates. It is an absolute absorption in the order of language and its poor relation to things: "Things present themselves in their stubborn existence, as if they were skilled in an ontological obstination which could shatter the most elementary rules of spatial distribution" (Foucault, 1992: 137). In Machery's estimation, the procedure "proves that there is no second language which would be the truth mirroring the first, but that the truth of language is entirely within itself, that is to say, in its indefinite proliferation" (1992: xxvi).

One might also add that it is the truth of things entirely within themselves that is apparent when Roussel gives us the space of the surface, things minutely documented in their exteriority. Arranged on the surface, things take on their full relations of proximity: "Their position is never defined in relation to the whole but according to a system of directions of proximity passing from one to the other…'to the left,' 'in front of them to the left,' 'above' …" (Foucault, cited in Philo, 1992: 145). And if this project sounds fussy, I wish to emphasize the mundane nature of such an enterprise, its very worldliness wherein sensuality, contingency, and particularity are played out in a so-what manner on the surface of things. It proposes a scheme of things resolutely without hierarchy; "posthumanist" *avant la lettre*, Roussel's depictions flatten out any possible normative distinction. As Chris Philo proposes in his reading of Foucault, Roussel, and Baudrillard, such attention awakens us to "the social world as a messy and...disordered geography of 'plates,' 'continents,' or 'fractal zones' slipping, sliding, and skidding into, under, and over one another" (1992: 158). For Philo, the attraction to the surface moves us away from "*depth* accounts of social life, where more fundamental levels of social reality (whether these be conceived of as economic, psychological, or whatever) are called upon to explain less fundamental ones" (1992: 158).

Here Philo catches the essence of the surface and why it is fundamentally important to cultural studies. For the surface is not another metaphor nor yet another fad within intellectual circles: it is a profound reordering of how we conceive of the social. In arguing for a conceptualization of belonging on the surface, I am arguing against marking identities within a hierarchical mode, whether the inner measure is oppression, domination, inequality, or whatever. As Bhabha states, the actual living of "the *locality* of culture," the articulation of cultural differences and identifications, should awaken us to the fact that it is always more complex "than can be represented in any hierarchical or binary structuring of social antagonism" (1994: 140). And it is deeply insufficient to think that we can comprehend forms of belonging by seeking to refer them to an underlying structuring principle, a stable and guaranteeing referent. At the same time that the "whatever" aspect of belonging on the surface forces us to relinquish the idea of guarding difference jealously as a personal possession whereby "my difference" makes me better than you, it also works against a happy pluralism. For the question of "being such that it always matters" constantly compels us within the processes of singularizing specificity. Conducted on the surface, this requires us to constantly place ourselves within relations of proximity of different forms of belonging. And at the edge of ourselves we mutate; we become other.

In more clear-cut terms, there are, I think, several exigencies demanded by this mode of theorizing. In no particular order, then, we might start with waking up to reality, that is, if we understand reality to be, as Lawrence Grossberg argues, "a structure of effects, marked by a multiplicity of planes and effects and the ways they intersect, transverse and disrupt each other" (1992: 48). And as I argue at some length in the final chapter, this is to consider, to take to heart, the task of being theorists on the outside, as translating across planes. Lest this language sound ephemeral, I should quickly add that this process of articulation on the surface demands a renewed rigor and awareness of the historicity of things, the ways in which the anteriority of things must be made to appear on their surface.

Surface belongings and desiring identities refuse to stand still; in-between being and longing, they compel connections, producing themselves as other. Such belonging is formulated in neither exclusionary nor inclusionary terms but in its sheer perplexity and yearning bypasses the meanness of individualized identities. Such forms of sociality, driven by desire, produce unexpected connections as they rub against each other, displaying on the surface their anteriority—the deep historicity of why, how, where, and with whom we may feel that we *belong*. Minute, meticulous, and mundane, these commonplace desires challenge me. If I propose the surface as a more adequate chronotope than models of depth and interiority, it is because I search not for causality but for transversal connections. Without falling into the trap of a realist epistemology or falling prey to delusions of omniscience, it is the search for surface connections that animates my thinking. And as I hope to show through the massive mobilization of small examples that fills the pages to follow, these desires for alternative relations and connections can only be considered superficial if seen through an optic that excludes their importance, puts them aside in the search for a deeper meaning. As the statement attributed to Freud (at least by generations of students) puts it, sometimes a cigar is just a cigar (which then makes the cigar all the more interesting).

Before turning to the next chapter, where I try to pry desire away from Freud and his followers, I add a final wish or warning. If the surface is but another optic, another way of viewing the social, it is only of use if it stretches our analytic reach, if it allows for other ways of seeing and connecting the various examples of our varied lives. If it encourages me to write from another angle, it is my hope that it also encourages a surface reading: a considered reading, but one which is interrupted by the reader's own examples, connections, and reconnections.

2

Becoming-Horse
Transports in Desire

becoming-horse

Getting Around

My mother had a passion for horses, one that she transmitted in different ways to her daughters, yet not to her son. In hindsight (and admittedly with a bit of filial licence), this passion could be seen as a longing for freedom, a desire to become other. Certainly some sort of yearning could be heard in a recurrent dream that she recounted to us several times during her life. She described it as located in a postapocalyptic time, after the dreaded bomb of the 1970s had been set off. In the dream, she hid from the devastation in an underground bunker with her favorite horse. When they finally ventured out they found a landscape devoid of any human feature, barren yet striking in its desolation. She then rode off across the land in the full knowledge that she and the horse would die because of this final but necessary ride. My mother always finished narrating the dream with a simple phrase: "Well, you know that I like horses better than people."

That at the time this didn't strike me as strange was in part because it was what I would have done, in part because of the context of the early 1970s and the pervasive fear that the world really would end. This fear was fueled by the low-flying American bomber jets that continually roared over the otherwise circumspect valleys of mid-Wales. Around that period my mother and I spent most of our time involved with horses. Having no money, she would find them on the cheap—at auctions where they were either classified as "aged" and fated for the glue factories in Belgium, or were psychologically abused creatures who had barely survived the patented cruel breaking methods of a prominent seller of horseflesh. If I grew up with pony-club stories about perfect little girls on their well-behaved mounts, the actuality was rather different. And if my mother dreamed of the upper-class hunts of the south of England, in our context riding was a rough passion, one that was addictive for the speed, the motion, the feeling of and the desire for being at the very edge of control: a wild running together of horse and girl.

Officially, my family's myth places us not with equus but under the sign of the train, recounting, recanting the story of my Canadian mother meeting a slightly hung-over British army officer on the CPR (the Canadian Pacific Railway Company). The story goes that she was leaving the West to get a job in External Affairs; he was brought over to teach Canadian soldiers home from the war how to parachute out of grain silos—a Cold War sort of thing. As the great train rolled on and on through the prairies, my mother's companion told her to offer that young man a drop of whisky. Three months later she was an army wife.

So, like most, I was born departing—watching from the sidelines the ways in which children seem to know as if by intuition who belongs and who doesn't. This then returns me to the principle of movement within belonging, and ways of getting about differently: movement that seeks not a straight path but rather revels in the inbetween, that picks up things along its way, that is derouted by small ethno-autobiographic shards—a tumbleweed of a theoretical project that gathers up memories, wishes, dreams, anecdotes, or sayings scribbled on city walls.

It seems to me that the processes of belonging are always tainted with deep insecurities about the possibility of truly fitting in, of even getting in. For example, I think of the wonderful Indo-Canadian film *Masala* (1993), where the stories of Indian immigrants who have "made good" in Canada play across the figure of the fully *Canadian* first-generation son. However, the representation of the son, Krishna, forefronts the inbetweenness of what it means to be Canadian, Indian, all portrayed in the shadows of planes that pass above him—planes that are for all in the film a constant reminder of the fatal Air India crash and the tragedy of Indians returning: returning to a home that is both India and Canada. *Masala* is exemplary in the way that it singularizes these specificities and makes clear that belonging is an inbetween state. It forefronts the ways in which these desires will always be diverse even as it catches at the immediacy of belonging, bringing forth images of leaving, carting one's possessions and baggage from place to place. Thus, while belonging may make one think of arriving, it also marks the often fearsome interstices of being and going, of longing, of not arriving.

Departing, getting going, going on, getting (it) on, getting by...these are necessary terms. They are also terms that I need to make rhyme with desire, a desire to keep on going, a desire to keep desire moving: a nebulous touch, a shifting of desire for a woman, a woman past and a woman present. These images of desire are not merely whimsical; rather, as concrete memories they embed themselves in the possibility of desire now. Images and fragments: meeting in a doorway, a handshake, a kiss, seeing my features rearranged as I smile back at her. Desire here is not metaphor; it is a method of doing things, of getting places. Desire here is the mode of connection and communication between things, inevitably giving way to the literalness of things.

Perhaps because I've never had a driver's licence, I've always been compelled by alternative modes of locomotion, modes such as horse-riding, biking, and swimming that will get you from point *a* to *b* but along the way will rearrange the pitch, the angle, and the perspective of the journey. They are also very embodied forms of transportation, forms that, after Deleuze, one could call modes of becoming, becoming-horse, becoming-bicycle, becoming-swimmer: the ways in which one becomes fully part of a machinery of movement—legs pumping, arms pulling, back straining, muscles melding. As Carol Anshaw writes in her novel on swimming and desire, it is an aquaphysics that can work only when the swimmer, the swimming, and the water become other than their separate functions: "She hyperventilates to expand her lungs, flattens her soles.... Now comes the critical moment, the one in which she needs to leave even herself behind and become purely what she can do, translate matter into energy, become velocity" (1993: 5). In theoretical terms, this idea of becoming-velocity can be situated within the realm of the spinozian-deleuzian, question not what is a body, but what can a body do? (Gatens, 1994; Grosz, 1994).

In this chapter I consider desire as movement; in particular, I want to raise the question of how we might formulate a singular and queer use of desire. To foreshadow the argument, I write against incarnating desire in an individual body in order to more fully realize the singular relations that are created through the movement of desire. This also entails reconsidering how we go about "interpreting" desire within a project of cultural criticism—to think of criticism as Rosi Braidotti does, as a process wherein "the category boundaries crumble away and writing and thought are conjugated together in a new relational mode" (1991: 280). I want to materialize desire as that productive force which compels a theory of belonging that in its singularity may exceed much of what passes for contemporary identity politics.

I should be clear that what I propose is only one possible line of analysis, a line that in turn meanders. I am fundamentally committed to a relational logic in making some relations clear, in making up others. That said, this is more of an exploration than an exposition of some hard-and-fast position. As a problematic, it is held together by the insistent and constant questioning of the singularity of belongings. If it is lesbian belonging that compels me here, it is only inasmuch as it is rendered singular, a singularity that cannot be posed in advance and that must not be posited as negating other singularities. If for reasons that are simultaneously personal, theoretical, and political I am drawn to figuring the singularity of lesbian-queer belonging, this cannot be seen as advocating an essential queerness. In any case, as I argued in the previous chapter, it is always a question of rendering zones of specificity into singularity, the force of desire to create and disrupt belonging. More specifically, this is to think not what is essential about desire, somehow located in something called a lesbian being, but rather how we engage in *manières*—manners of being expressed in small movements of belonging—the singular "so-whatness" of desire as lines of connection and communication between beings, ways of being, and things.

This brings to the fore the problem of figuring that movement. To use a term that has become problematic, how do we go about "representing" desire? Given my formation in communication studies, this leads me to think about the place of desire in models of communication, representation, and interpretation. While the interconnection of communication, transport, movement, and desire may be an idiosyncratic one, it is not overly far-fetched. These terms share a similar relational motive; they are all about tracing lines between different points. Too often, they are used to designate an end point, but they can also be used to think about the inbetweenness that they fundamentally suggest. So these terms are not communication as privileging the final reception, not transport as arriving at the terminus, and certainly not desire as located in an object; rather, they may point us to moments of being—like the moment when the trapeze artist has let go of one ring but hasn't yet grasped the other.[1] This is an image of momentum and chance that captures for me what belonging is all about. While it may or may not be a scary image (think of how audiences gasp, all the while knowing that she will grasp the other ring), I use it to remind myself of a sense of precariousness that is necessarily part of our being and belonging and that should be included in our theories.

For desire is a profoundly upsetting force. It may totally rearrange what we think we want: desire skews plans, setting forth unthought-of possibilities. But, as a term within traditional models of communication, desire has tended to reassure the established order of things. It has either been totally missing or has served to operate as the ever unattainable referent: the lack that guarantees signification, a lack that is traditionally figured as woman or other. As Grossberg argues, accepted models of communication assume "a relationship between two discrete and independently existing entities: whether between individuals, or between audiences and texts, or between signifieds and signifiers" (1992: 38). This organization of the communication process is most evident within poststructuralist readings of communication and culture: "The terms of the communicative relationship—the very existence of texts, meanings and audiences—are themselves the result of the continuous production of difference, the gap, between them" (Grossberg, 1992: 40). Here desire as lack is the oblique term that nonetheless sustains such structures and works to produce a conception of the social which Félix Guattari categorizes as "a tripartition between a field of reality, the world, a field of representation, the book, and a field of subjectivity, the author" (cited in Grossberg, 1992: 48).

This divvying up of the social can be heard in any number of oppositions which pose modes of knowing through the logic of signifier to signified. And between the two terms yawns a gap, a frightening abyss that leads to a reification of the signifier and a fetishization of the gap—the lack of correspondence that assures meaning. It is as if, deeply perturbed by the ways in which things don't meet up with words, we construct their point of missing as a structural lack, a teleology fueled by sheer impossibility. As Foucault so clearly reminds us, "in every society the production of discourse is at once controlled, selected, organized and redistributed by a certain number of procedures which have the role of exorcising powers and dangers, of mastering hazardous events, of dodging the heavy, the fearsome materiality" (1971: 10–11). Cliché though it may be, one can't help but feel that at play here is the specter of the very possibility of the meaninglessness of life. In Nietzsche's words, having moved from irrationality, "now as a '*rational*' being [man] submits his actions to the sway of abstractions; he no longer suffers himself to be carried away by sudden abstractions, by sensations, he first generalizes all these impressions into paler cooler ideas, in order to attach to them the slip of his life and actions" (1972: 6).

It is the slip of life and actions, the slip between being and longing, that we paste over, that we search to avoid when we erect an edifice of communication based in lack. As Grossberg argues, "What is crucial here is the rejection of the model of culture defined by the need to construct a correspondence between two parallel, nonintersecting planes—language and reality" (1992: 48). These planes are held apart, their frightening discursive materiality controlled, through the supposition of desire as lack. This structuration then plays out in the search to separate different orders, to fixate on some principle that would guarantee meaning in chaos. How else to explain the bizarre displays of enunciation within the sphere of identity politics whereby "difference" is performed as highly individualized: "*my* difference as a _____," as somehow terrifyingly fragile and competitive, as if your difference will nullify mine.

A refusal of this logic whereby difference is always accompanied by the other as "my" lack can be clearly heard in Deleuze and Guattari's argument against the laws of signification, "the three errors of lack, law and signifier": "It is one and the same error, an idealism that forms a pious conception of the unconscious.... From the moment lack is reintroduced into desire, all of desiring production is crushed, reduced to being no more than the production of fantasy; but the sign does not produce fantasies, it is a production of the real and a position of desire within reality" (cited in Grossberg, 1992: 49–51). At once so simple and so evident, the idea that desire produces within the real—indeed produces the real—is also a veritable rupture with many modes of conceptualizing being in the world. Desire as fully social encourages a mode of thinking in which "events have to be taken literally, in the facticity of their singular existence, rather than as texts to be interpreted" (Grossberg, 1992: 49). This conception of desire begs the difficult questions that Agamben poses: "How is it possible to speak without presupposing, without hypothesizing and subjectivizing or subjecting what one speaks about? How is it possible not to speak *on* the presupposition of a thing, but to say *the thing itself?*" (1987: 23). While these are open if not impossible questions, they direct me to ways of connecting or of entering into things, becoming-things rather than seeking their deep, discrete, inherent meaning. The thing itself is to be found on the surface along with other things, their meaning only to be found in how they may or may not connect.

In tracing out lines of belonging I am interested in how they may converge, their principle being one of desire that *translates across*, "desire circulating in this arrangement of heterogeneity, in this space of 'symbiosis': desire being one with the arrangement of heterogeneity, a co-functioning" (Deleuze, 1994: 60). In refusing to distinguish between the social and the symbolic, the real and the discursive, this is to render desire as entirely social, as lubricating lines of governance and power, and those of subjectification. This is clearly heard in the terms that Deleuze uses to talk about the arrangements of desire, or rather "l'agencement de désir"—desire as engaging in the way that gears are engaged and engage each other. This engagement brings together heterogeneous orders of things: "For example, feudalism is an *agencement* which put into play new relations between the animal (the horse), the land, deterritorialization (horse racing, the Crusade), women (chivalrous love)…etc." (Deleuze, 1994: 60).

Queer Points of Departure

Horses, planes, and trains…strange points of departure. As objects, they seem so impossibly phallic, already trapped within disciplinary sets of luggage, epistemological belongings. I think of how Raymond Bellour interpreted the horse in Hitchcock's film *Marnie*. Against the wealth of possibilities suggested by the sumptuous shots of Marnie and her horse, Bellour argues that "Marnie's fetishistic love for Forio…typically takes the place of a man and children" (1977: 84). It is an interpretation that can only be conducted from within the safe framework of psychoanalytic film theory, one that in this case misses Hitchcock's incredible *mise-en-scène* of Marnie's desire. Think of the close-ups of Marnie caressing her horse as he responds; consider her impassioned plea, "Oh, Forio, if you want to bite someone, bite *me*"; and recall the long shots of woman and animal blurred together across the landscape. Faced with all this, Bellour manages to doubly take away Marnie's pleasure with her horse when he posits that on the one hand, it is merely the "pleasure of the signified…the horse, animality, the phallic substitute" and on the other, this image is "the condition necessary to the constitution of [Hitchcock's] phantasy" (1977: 85–86). In this interpretation, the image of the horse impales desire as the desire for the phallus, and, in the case of *Marnie*, for the family. It cannot be Marnie's desire; it always-already displaces hers as the condition of another's desire.

As condensed as Bellour's reading may seem, it is hard to escape psychoanalytic interpretations of desire. In fact, it may be that other approaches to culture have shied away from the notion precisely because of psychoanalytic cultural criticism's hold on desire. In turn, and given the pervasiveness of psychoanalytically influenced readings, it is not surprising that, with notable exceptions, psychoanalytic assumptions either inform or creep into considerations of queer desire. This then plays out in a tendency to individualize desire and erects an "other" in order to secure meaning. As Biddy Martin argues, the "other" often comes as either woman or feminism. While convinced of the potential of queer studies, Martin states, "I am worried when antifoundationalist celebrations of queerness rely on their projections of fixity, constraint, or subjection onto a fixed ground, often onto feminism or the female body, in relation to which queer sexualities become figural, performative, playful, and fun" (1994: 104). Here feminism is objectified and found lacking, just as it is forced to perform the role of the necessary lack. This is certainly not to say that queer theorists avoid lesbians—on the contrary, as lesbians we have never been so courted—it's just that some theorists (male, female, and transgender) are made distinctly uneasy when the lesbian comes as feminist; with or without dildo, she becomes the dreaded figure of castration and lack.

Although, for many reasons, I have not taken the time necessary to fit in with feminist psychoanalytic theory, I am impressed by those who have. I am even more impressed by those who have possessed this machine, who made it belong to them and for them, only to depart from it. They also tend to be rare. A case in point is Elizabeth Grosz, who a few years ago and after years of working through Lacan, up and left psychoanalysis. The move seems to be simple, even if the logistics of leaving probably were not: "I don't want to talk about lesbian psychologies, about the psychical genesis of lesbian desire. . . . I am much less interested in where lesbian desire comes from, how it emerges, and the ways in which it develops than where it is going to, its possibilities, its open-ended future" (1994a: 68–69).

In that my argument is not against psychoanalysis but rather for another use of desire, I will not enter into a discussion of the strengths and limits of psychoanalytic cultural criticism.[2] Rather, I want to rework desire in order to lose the points of arrival that are imbricated in it. As one of my points of departure, I turn to Deleuze, who reads desire through and in tension with Foucault. As Foucault and Deleuze's exchange makes clear, the very word encapsulates tenacious tendencies: Deleuze recalls Foucault saying to him "with much kindness and affection.... I cannot stand the word desire; even if you use it differently, I can't help myself thinking or living desire = lack, or that desire says repression" (1994: 63).

To briefly map out the terms of their disagreement, Foucault sees desire as a contaminated term; at one point, he argues that "desire is not an event but a permanent feature of the subject: it provides a basis onto which all that psychologico-medical armature can attach itself" (cited in Halperin, 1995: 94). In the stead of desire, Foucault turns to "pleasure," in part due to the fact that it "is virgin territory, unused, almost devoid of meaning. There is no 'pathology' of pleasure, no 'abnormal' pleasure" (cited in Halperin, 1995: 94). While this distinction seems clear cut, in his later work Foucault studies how sexual practices and pleasures were problematized in order to analyze the ways in which Western man has constituted himself as a subject of desire. In a sense, one could say that Foucault's analyses of desire allow us to now return to the term, that it has been rid of naturalized connotations and pathologizing motives. In any case, and in combination with Deleuze's effort to free desire from its institutionalized moorings, it seems rather unproductive to maintain a categorical refusal of the concept. For example, in his book on Foucault, David Halperin states, "Unlike desire, which expresses the subject's individuality, history, and identity as a subject, pleasure is desubjectivating, impersonal: it shatters identity, subjectivity, and dissolves the subject, however fleetingly, into the sensorial continuum of the body, into the unconscious dreaming of the mind" (1995: 95). In that Halperin's book bypasses Deleuze and is also nearly devoid of recent feminist foucauldian work on the body, it is perhaps inevitable that Foucault's complicated relationship between desire, pleasure, bodies, and power should be reduced to the sensory body on the one hand and the dreaming mind on the other.

Halperin's remarks follow from Foucault's discussion of the pleasures of gay male sex, in particular the s/m practices that flourished in the bath houses of the 1970s. While these examples are illuminating, Halperin makes a direct equation between marginalization and queer, arguing, "to marginalize: that is, *to queer*" (1995: 111). If we invert the equation: to queer, that is to say, to marginalize, we find ourselves back in the thick of celebratory queer cultural theories whereby mainstream cultural icons are queered and rendered deviant. Even as he refuses to see the positivity of desire (and the positivity of Foucault's use of positivity), Halperin's argument is animated by an unproblematized notion of marginality, individuality, and sexual pleasure as resistance. Strangely enough, in his enthusiasm for Foucault, Halperin comes close to precisely reterritorializing "pleasure" in much the way that Deleuze warns against.

To continue with the terms of the desire-pleasure debate, Deleuze maintains that it is precisely pleasure that "interrupts the positivity of desire." Pleasure operates a "re-territorialization"; it disarms desire within a "grid of identifications" (Massumi, 1992: 51), and "in this way, desire is returned to the law of lack and to the norm of pleasure" (Deleuze, 1994: 64). If Foucault's notion of pleasure coexists with a deleuzian understanding of desire, it seems to me that the latter extends the former as it passes through Foucault's theorization of power and subjectification. For desire is central to Deleuze's notion of the lines of flight, key to thinking about how to conceive of relations, conjugations, conjunctures in a logic of de-routing the reterritorialization, the setting of normalized ways of being. And it must be noted that this re-territorialization of desire into norm can proceed at many levels: evidently through state and social sanctions of "normal" heterosexuality but also through the setting up of territorialized modes of *being* gay, lesbian, queer, or whatever. In the face of the tendency for sexuality to be thus reduced, recaptured, Deleuze again returns to the movement of desire, to see "sexuality as engagement [*l'agencement*] of desire historically variable and determinable, with its points of deterritorialization, of flux and of combination" (1994: 64). Thus, as a problematic, desire compels me to work along the lines constantly set off between and among longing, leaving, being, bodies, images, movement. It should also cause us to be wary of reterritorializing any practice (be it queer or other).

If, as Deleuze says, Foucault's "idea that apparatuses of power have an immediate and direct relation with the body is essential" (1994: 64),

equally important is the framework that Deleuze gives to study the relation of desire and the composition of the social. To very roughly sketch out
the connections, for Deleuze, "a society, the field of the social does not
contradict itself, but first and foremost, it flees...[and] the lines of flight
constitute the rhizome or the cartography" (1994: 62). Lines of flight are
then the engagements of desire, desire which is "only defined by zones of
intensity, thresholds, gradients and flux." In turn, it is across bodies ("a
body that is biological as well as collective and political") that these engagements are made and unmade; "it is [the body] which carries the points of
deterritorialization of the engagements [of desire] or the lines of flight"
(1994: 63): not *my* body but *a* body.

Deleuze's thought gives flesh to an intuition that desire can be used
to scramble traditional thresholds between the social and the subjective:
"It is in this sense that desire seems to me foremost, and to be the element
of a micro-analysis" of the social (Deleuze, 1994: 61). Grosz's chapter on
Deleuze and Guattari in her book *Volatile Bodies* is a clear exposition of what
she calls "unexpectedly powerful weapons of analysis." As she argues,
"Desire does not take for itself a particular object whose attainment it
requires; rather, it aims at nothing above its own proliferation or self-
expansion. It assembles things out of singularities and breaks things, assemblages, down into their singularities. It moves; it does." (1994a: 165). This
conception of desire is especially exciting for feminist analyses of the materiality of the body as it frees women from being positioned and objectified
as the "guardians of the lack constitutive of desire...insofar as the opposition between presence and absence, reality and fantasy, has traditionally
defined and constrained woman to inhabit the place of man's other"
(Grosz, 1994a: 165).

This deleuzian conception of desire and movement "demassifies" the
body: "Bodies are defined not by their genus and species, nor by their origins and functions, but by what they can do, the effects they are capable of,
in passion as in action" (Deleuze and Parnet, 1987, cited in Grosz, 1994a:
169). Bodies, and desire, are only of interest inasmuch as they engage with
others. Simply put, a body, moved by desire, propels itself into networks
and milieux of bodies and things. In turn, the milieu must be conceived of
as a dynamic arena of social action. In Deleuze's description, "a milieu is
made of qualities, substances, forces and events: for example, the street

with its matter like paving-stones, its noises like the cry of the merchants, its animals like the horses yoked, its dramas (a horse slips, a horse falls, a horse is beaten…)" (1993: 81). As a concept, the milieu begins here to take on its full importance: it is the ground of desire, a ground that must be rendered in the very detail of its singular qualities.

Deleuze's description of milieu comes from his article "Ce que disent les enfants" (1993), a profound rereading of Freud's "Little Hans," perhaps the casebook study of Oedipal fixing. Deleuze frees Little Hans from his position as belonging to Freud and to the history of psychoanalysis, which he characterizes as this "rage of possessiveness and of the personal [in which psychoanalytic] interpretation consists in finding the person and his possessions" (1993: 86). He looses Little Hans from the grip of Freudian principles and lets him once again wander the streets, his desire to meet up with the rich little girl taking him by the horses' stable. Deleuze argues that Freud reduces this meandering "to the father-mother: bizarrely enough, the wish to explore the building strikes Freud as the desire to sleep with the mother" (1993: 81). Instead of desire thus fixed and identified, Deleuze proposes a cartographic logic whereby "maps superimpose…it is not a question of looking for an origin, but rather of evaluating *displacements*" (1993: 83–84).

In Deleuze's retelling of Little Hans' story one can glimpse another mode of reading, or interpretation, even as these terms are proven inadequate. For if interpretation presupposes an inner meaning, here Deleuze undoes the elements that Freud has knotted together in his moral tale. As Grosz puts it, "a Deleuzian model insists on the flattening out of relations between the social and the psychical so that there is neither a relation of causation (one- or two-way) nor hierarchies, levels, grounds, or foundations. The social is not privileged over the psychical…nor is the psychical privileged at the expense of the social" (1994: 180). In Deleuze's own terms, "The pharaoh's tomb, with its inert central room at the bottom of the pyramid, gives way to more dynamic models: from the drift of continents to the migration of peoples, the means by which the unconscious maps the universe" (1993: 84).[3] At one level, Deleuze frees up the richness of the psychic and the social precisely by refusing to give them dichotomous standing. In discussing Little Hans' affective universe, Deleuze states that it would be abusive to see as Freud does, a simple derivation of the father-mother: "as if the 'vision' of the street, frequent at the time—a horse falls, is beaten, struggles—wasn't capable of directly affecting the libido, and has to recall his parents having sex" (1993: 84). On another level, "the identification of the horse with the father touches on the grotesque, and carries a misunderstanding of all the connections the unconscious has with animal forces" (84).

It is not that the little boy transposes the horse (with its *grand fait-pipi*) onto the father, nor is it that horse has some mythical standing; rather, in a common way, Little Hans becomes-horse, entailing an "intensity which distributes affects, the liaison, the valency, which constitute each time the image of the body, an image always reworkable or transformable in relation to the affective constellations that determine it" (Deleuze, 1993: 85). Becoming-horse thus designates a moment of valency and of micro-combination between the image the boy has of his body *in relation* to the horse. This inbetween moment should not be misunderstood as a simple projection onto horse of being a horse but rather entails a certain dissolution of the body-image as known, as *my* body, in favor of another image, that of becoming-horse. This becoming involves "a kind of wildness, pivots of unpredictability, elements whose trajectories, connections, and future relations remain unpredictable" (Grosz, 1994a: 174). Although it could suggest a certain romanticism of becoming one with the animal, it is, in Deleuze's description, a rudely impersonal state: "It is the determination of becoming, its proper power, the power of an impersonal which is not a generality, but a singularity at its highest: for example, one does not do *the* horse, no more than one imitates *such* a horse, but one becomes *a* horse, in attaining a zone of proximity where one can no longer distinguish from what one becomes" (1993: 86). Elsewhere, Deleuze and Guattari describe how "the actor Robert de Niro walks 'like' a crab in a certain film sequence; but, he says, it is not a question of his imitating a crab; it is a question of making something that has to do with the crab enter into composition with the image, with the speed of the image" (cited in Grosz, 1994a: 226).

While these processes of becoming obviously carry profound implications for how we consider questions of subjectivity, individuality, and the makeup of the social world, I want to turn to the more precise question of Deleuze's mode of retelling the story of Little Hans' adventures. It strikes me that as he gives us an account of Little Hans becoming-horse, we can also see Deleuze becoming–Little Hans. Beyond the ordinary sense of interpretation and its limiting connotations, Deleuze describes and becomes the boy within the machinations of all the elements of his milieu. This is not to say that he empathizes with the boy; rather, Deleuze *displaces* Little Hans, and that displacement mobilizes the milieu in all of its social, psychic, animal elements, freeing up lines of movement, sounds and tangibilities. Becoming–Little Hans–becoming-horse entails a running together and a flattening out of these elements. As Grosz says of the deleuzian "framework" (as she too perhaps strives to find a term more adequate than "representation" or "interpretation"), "this means that individuals, subjects, microintensities, blend with, connect to, neighborhood, local, regional, social, cultural, aesthetic, and economic relations directly, not through mediation of systems of ideology or representation" (1994a: 180).

If we cannot, strictly speaking, talk of a deleuzian "interpretation" (unless it be something like Glenn Gould's machinic "interpretation" of becoming-Bach), Deleuze has delved into the style of several philosophers and of philosophy itself. As he makes clear in a discussion of Spinoza, style is to be understood as encompassing "three poles, the concept or new ways of thinking, the percept or new ways of seeing and hearing, the affect or new ways of experiencing" (1990: 224). In a rather remarkable text that opens *Pourparlers* ("Lettre à un critique sévère"), Deleuze speaks of what it is to write and to read: "To write, is a flow amongst others, and one which has no privilege in relation to others, and which enters relations of current, of counter-current, of eddies with other flows, flows of shit, of sperm, of words, of action, of eroticism, of money, of politics, etc." (1990: 17–18). And of reading, he writes: "This manner of reading in intensity, in relation with the outside, flow against flow, machine with machines, experimentations, events which for each has nothing to do with the book, the shredding of the book, making it function with other things, whatever…, etc., this is a way of [being in] love" ("une manière amoureuse") (1990: 18).

What I take from this discussion is another mode of going about figuring relations: a manner of cultural criticism (for lack of a better word) committed to putting desire to work, to the tangibility of milieu, to putting the elements of the milieu into flight, to becoming that which one describes in becoming. While this is not a new idea *per se* (Foucault always maintained that one writes in order to become other, in order to lose oneself), it demands an absolute commitment to attention and acuity. It is also, as should be very clear, a resolutely impersonal and depersonalizing mode. And it is perhaps here that the real difficulty lies: for even as I am compelled to document, observe, watch for small lines of flight, minute instances of inbetweenness that signal a becoming-other, there cannot be a return to an elevated, authorial perspective. That personage, as we might agree, has for too long stood on a conception of the other, my other, held in place as the lack. Rather than a relation of alterity, the mode I am suggesting seeks to provoke other relations of proximity, effects which Deleuze describes as "shadows on the surface of bodies, always between two bodies…It is always a body that casts shadow on the other" (1990: 175). Taking from Bergson (as Deleuze does), this is to reconceive of the body as image, as "the *place of passage* of the movements received and thrown back, a hyphen, a connecting link between things which act upon me and the things upon which I act" (cited in Massumi, 1992: 185).

An example of the ways in which images connect with bodies in order to enjoin other images can be heard in a weird little exchange between Foucault and Hélène Cixous. In it, and *avant la lettre*, they queer images arising from Marguerite Duras's *Moderato Cantabile*. The image of a breast brings Foucault to talk about the movement of *la drôlerie* (which may come closer to being a French translation of queer than would Sedgwick's *troublant* [1993: xii]). Cixous then defines the breast in relation to "the image…a regard [a look] of such extreme intensity" (1975: 10). For Foucault, the relation between the image and the gaze of the looker is rendered "drôle…in the sense of something strange, avid, not quite graspable" (1975: 10).

In this sense, images are only queer inasmuch as they are avid for relations that seek other relations. For if the queer image does indeed do something, it is in its capacity for connecting and reconnecting relations (sexual and other). The singularity of queer desire may reside in the ways in which it puts the body, bodies, and bits of bodies to work hyphenating connections. The momentum here is rhizomatic, with stems of images carrying both their roots and shoots; the image constantly turns itself inside out. Or, as Foucault put it in one of his rare comments on lesbians, "sexual relations are immediately transferred into social relations and the social relations are understood as sexual relations" (1989: 272).

Elspeth Probyn

Girls and Girls and Horses

As I think about how images may reconnect in other ways, an image passes: of girlfriends melded together by hot horseflesh, bodies strung together by the smell of elderflower branches slapping away the flies. The identity of the individual bodies is of little interest; rather, it is the way in which they are held together by a singular girl-practice of becoming-horse: a milieu of becoming-horse, becoming-woman that is constituted within the changing elements of sociality and bodies.

I am, of course, far from alone in thinking that there is something wonderfully thrilling about the movement of women on women on horses. From *National Velvet* to *My Friend Flicka*, horses figure in film in any number of ways. More often than not, the images in these horse films concern the strength of females. For example, the young Liz Taylor sets out to win the Grand National not to secure Micky Rooney's heart but to continue a line of physical feats that runs from her mother's attempts to swim the English Channel. The desire to become-horse is unmistakable in scenes that show Liz in her bed repeating and caught up in the motion of riding, her arms stretched forward, her legs straining. As with Deleuze and Guattari's description of De Niro's crab, these shots catch the lines of flight between girl and horse and dwell on the inbetweenness of two machinic entities.

In turn, these images play back and forth within a milieu of girls, allowing them to engage with the composition and the momentum of the image. This becoming-horse has little to do with actually having a horse; rather, it is a current within the structure of girls' lives, a moment that is characterized by a tremendous experimentation of images, especially those of one's own body. At least in our society, young girls are particularly focused as the site of reception of images. And while too often it is a site that is pathologized,[4] more attention should be paid to the ways in which bodies become hyphens for connecting various images, a swapping ground for different imaginary maps and cards of what one is becoming. Instead of rendering this inbetweenness pathological in its nonunity, we need to consider the open possibilities enacted within a milieu of connecting body parts (my emerging breasts against yours). There is a moment in the social structuration of girlhood when one may feel with great acuity "the production of intricate machinic connections which distribute intensities across bodies and objects, experimenting with the plane of consistency of desire itself" (Grosz, 1994a: 226). The images of girls and horses then play within this, creating and allowing for lines of desire that connect elsewhere and in other ways.

Contra Bellour, and others who would see in the attraction of horses but a rehearsal for the "big event," one could say that in the eyes of Marnie, Sean Connery was merely a poor substitute for her horse Forio, or that it is the man who gains from the horse and not the other way around. In any case, the milieu of horses is for the most part a female domain. As far as I remember from the pony-club stories and experiences of my youth, it was always girls and girls and horses together, with nary a boy in sight. Within popular culture this generalized coupling of girls and horses ("pony mad") then operates in opposition to that of girls and boys ("boy crazy") in order to produce a normative sexual structure of femininity. But equine associations vary, and they always implicate other social structures. For instance, while in other parts of the world British horsiness is seen as middle or upper class, horses in the rough farming region of my childhood did not constitute a status symbol, and ours in particular certainly couldn't have been considered as such. This is not to suggest a demarcation between the lived and images—in my own concrete example, images from elsewhere played alongside "real" horses, as when girlfriends from town came out to our village to ride out their fantasies on my unwilling nag. Images take off from lived singularities just as they feed into them. And virtual images of horses have traveled widely, and indeed have been an effective strategy of British colonization (of lands and girls). Be it in India, Canada, or Australia, wherever girls' horse stories have landed, they aid and abet a certain structuring of femininity, social class, and the establishment of a structure of feeling of young girls' sexuality, even as they may be put to work to deterritorialize these structures.

It should be equally obvious that not all girls are interested in the processes of becoming-horse, processes that cannot be generalized, just as their directions cannot be assumed in advance. Within certain milieux, at certain times, images may be pried loose from a more conventional mooring and catch up certain bodies in lines of becoming. But, as Deleuze argues following Spinoza, they "*do not have objects as their direct referent. It is the state of bodies* (affections) and the variations of force (affects) which send them off one to another.... They have for referent a disordered mélange of bodies and obscure variations of force, following an order which is that of Chance or a fortuitous encounter between bodies" (1993: 175). In this vein, images of girls and girls and horses have no referent other than the mélange of bodies and affections that may send them off.

If the ordering logic is one of chance or of fortuitous encounters following the vagaries of desire, there is a historicity to the milieu in which they play. There is an archive of the connections between girls and horses: a repertoire of images of women-becoming-horse, images of the connection, and images that continue to forge other connections. One of my favorites comes from Colette, a writer who has inspired many women in becoming-cat. In *The Pure and the Impure*, Colette strings together a series of impressions recalling what she calls "the noble season of feminine passion." The book, which was first privately published in 1932 as *Ces plaisirs* after her phrase "Ces plaisirs qu'on nomme, à la légère, physique" ("These pleasures which are lightly called physical"), is a marvelous feat of writing and one that catches at and is caught up in various forms of becoming. Consider what she says of her account of the long-lived love of Lady Eleanor Butler and Miss Sarah Ponsonby, the Ladies of Llangollen: "How reluctant I am to handle dispassionately anything in creation as perilously fragile as an amorous ménage of two women!"—a ménage she then describes as composed of a "roof unstable and immaterial, shored up by apposed foreheads, clasped hands, united lips" (1971: 91). Bits of bodies float throughout and are connected and reconnected through passion and desire—desire for other women and passion for writing: "I resumed my post at the side of the worktable, where my woman's eyes followed, on the pale blue bonded paper, the hard and stubby hand of a gardener writing" (59).

Colette's writing is exemplary in its depiction of milieu. She traces the ways in which lines of desire flow and are slowed by the redirections of social status and enforced gender, only to resume again in another corner where "once the slow-thinking male had been banished, every message from woman to woman became clear and overwhelming, restricted to a small but infallible number of signs" (69). While there are references to horsewomen scattered throughout, one of the more compelling chapters traces the figure of "La Chevalière." Colette recalls how La Chevalière gathered together a medley of women from the highest strata of society who, smelling of "the exciting scent of horses...tried to render intelligible for us their success with women and their defiant taste for women" (65–66). These *fin-de-siècle* Parisian butches joined their taste for women with an appreciation of horseflesh. Colette revels in the milieu composed of women, class, desire, scent, and style: "Some of them wore a monocle, a white carnation in the button-hole, took the name of God in vain, and discussed horses competently. These mannish women I am calling to mind were, indeed, almost as fond of the horse, that warm, enigmatic, stubborn and sensitive creature, as they were of their young protégées" (65).

For her time, and due in part to her own upbringing, Colette is remarkably sensitive to the class differences that pervade this horsy set. When she writes that "these ladies in male attire had, by birth and from infancy, a taste for below-stairs accomplices and comrades-in-livery" (63), she also details the lines of desire that connected women of such different social status. In the tradition of the time and class, as young girls the aristocratic women had been given over by their parents to servants, to fit in "downstairs" as they might. From their childhoods spent within the complicated lines of power, class position, gender, and desire, "these women who had been dispossessed of their rightful childhoods and who, as girls, had been little more than orphans, were now in their maturity the fond instructors of a younger generation" (65). In a tableau that traces the lines of flight from the assemblages of forced marriages, orphaned childhoods, and rigid femininity, Colette writes of a generation of women like La Chevalière, who "most often bruised herself in a collision with a woman— a woman, that whispering guide, presumptuous, strangely explicit" (68). As she mourns the passing of these women, she eulogizes their equestrienne, lesbienne existence: "The dust of the bridle paths in the Bois still haloes, in countless memories, these equestriennes who did not need to ride astride to assert their ambiguity" (69). From her description, we can hear a seamless articulation of horses, bodies, and lesbian desire that allowed these women to move gracefully outside heterosexual clumsiness, the transition from pedestrian butch to the state of fluidity; once "mounted on the twin pedestal of a chestnut crupper...they were freed of the awkward, toed-out stance of the ballet dancer that marred their walk" (69).

If, in Colette's description, lesbian desire flows more freely once mounted, in *The Well of Loneliness* we have quite another set of images of bodies exchanged in desire. Yet, in their singularity, they too cross the bodies of a horse and a woman. Indeed, Radclyffe Hall goes further than La Chevalière and effectively transubstantiates the body of Stephen Gordon's first object of desire, Collins, the housemaid (again "below-stairs"), into that of her first horse: "Laying her cheek against his firm neck, she said softly: 'You're not *you* any more, you're Collins'" (1968: 42). As Hall puts it, "Collins was comfortably transmigrated."

These are for me singular images that raise the movements of desire that are exchanged through horses, small glimpses of becoming-horse, becoming-woman. For instance, in Hall's account, horse, desire, and woman are folded upon themselves as body upon body converse "in a quiet language having very few words but many small sounds and many small movements, that meant much more than word" (cited in Whitlock, 1987: 571). As Alison Hennegan aptly states, it is a "description that can easily apply to satisfactory love-making" (cited in Whitlock, 1987: 571).

Now, in that Hall's championing of theories of inversion are well known, some might be tempted to say that this equine transubstantiation of her lover for her horse translates as a psychological substitution of the lover for the horse and hence for the phallus. However, Hall's reading of Havelock Ellis's theories on sexuality also puts lesbian desire within the natural order. As Jean Radford argues, "her inverted love is God-given, [but] she is not, it seems, allowed to enjoy it" (1986: 107). If she cannot take pleasure in her God-given desire, thanks to her social position, she is allowed to enjoy her love for Collins through her horse. Hall's use of the horse enacts another becoming-horse whereby the horse, the lover, and Stephen partially dissolve in order to reconnect in another direction, one that fulfills for Hall her desire for women. For us it may be a rather tortuous route, but given the milieu in which it is performed, it makes a certain sense. Thus, within the social restraints of her time, Hall reconnects her "natural" state of inversion with an object of nature in order to consummate her love. Drawn on by desire, in the novel horse and lover are made to intersect at Stephen's body, refracted off Hall's body clothed in the scientific theories of her time and masculine riding outfits.

These are, of course, selective examples taken from a repertoire that could include many others (there is a wide and seemingly endless variety of equine connections and reconnections). These images of girls and girls and horses cannot have an essence, or fixed reference; set off in tandem with one body, they may or may not meet up and touch off desire in another's. Within an alternative mode of cultural interpretation, clearly it makes no sense to read these images as tied down in a relationship of signifier to signified, nor is it satisfying to pin them as fixed referents of the phallus. Along the same line, I would be hard put to argue that they have an intrinsic, inherent *lesbian* meaning. Rather, what is interesting here, and indeed striking, is the way in which they move as lines of desire between lesbians and horses and lesbians. Equally, they must be read as initiating altered and alternative relations within a matrix of class, race, and ethnicity as well as sexuality.

While they cannot be allowed to condense into categorized notions of being, they can, however, carry longing; they throw us forward into other relations of becoming and belonging. Nicole Brossard articulates this idea in a rather more elegant way when she writes that "the image is a vital resource that forms complex propositions from simple and isolated elements. Each time an image relays desire, this image thinks, with unsuspected vitality, the drift of meaning. So it is that images penetrate the solid matter of our ideas without our knowledge" (1991: 196). Taking up mundane fragments in its movement, the image is riven by desire, the desire to become other, a machinery of horse and lesbian desiring. For example, in a poem by Ruthann Robson, an image of a "stampede of wild horses" carries the narrator forward into a realization "that what you want is to become." And what she wants to become is caught up in the image of "two women without berets...two mares at the river" (1992: 110). Or again, in Anzaldúa's story of a woman who finally realizes she can love her lover, the final image is one of how "It would start here. She would eat horses, she would let horses eat her" (1990: 388).

The image, thus freed from its post within a structure of law, lack, and signification, can begin to move all over the place. It then causes different ripples and affects, effects of desire and desirous affects. Turning away from the game of matching signifiers to signifieds, we can begin to focus on the movement of images as effecting and affecting movement. As Grosz has argued, this is "to look at lesbian relations and, if possible, all social relations in terms of bodies, energies, movements, inscriptions rather than in terms of ideologies, the inculcation of ideas, the transmission of systems of belief or representations" (1994b: 77–78).

By way of horses and lesbians and becoming-horse, I wish to suggest that the image becomes that with which we think and feel our way from body to body, as vectors thrust forward by the energies created in their different relations of proximity and distance. Becoming as that inbetween moment, the disengagement and re-engaging of different parts cannot be about policing images for their content. In Brossard's essay of unraveling desire in "the green night of labyrinth park," she wonders whether "in the very carnal night of solstice, is the image lesbian because in reproducing it I want it to be so?" (1991: 196). This is a tricky point in that in part it *is* through the desire that it be so, a desire aimed at making it so. While the idea that the image is lesbian because I want it to be so may smack of either wishful thinking or voluntarism, Brossard reminds us that this wishfulness may be actualized only through the force of desire and the ways in which images are reproduced. These hopeful lesbian images (images that we wish were lesbian) work not in relation to any supposed point of authenticity but in their transversal movement, in the ways in which they set up relational lines of desire. The image is lesbian only inasmuch as it allows for carnal lines of connection, the way it engages desire and the way in which desire moves it. To be absolutely clear about it, the image is queer not in and of itself but in relation to other images and bodies—a movement that refuses to be policed at the same time that it says come to me, as it bends the line, causing changed relations of proximity. As Brossard writes, "The image slips, surprising re/source that slips endlessly through meanings, seeking the angle of thoughts in the fine moment where the best of intentions guiding me, worn out by repetition, seem about to close in silently on themselves. [But] the image persists.... It goes against chance, fervent relay" (1991: 196). In Brossard's description we feel the full force of the image, the hope that it carries in its subjunctive fashion, that movement of desire when desire questions itself: Is she looking at me? Is she interested? Is she available? (Or, as a Swiss friend used to say, "Does she have the same life as us?") The image teeters, skitters between despair and longing; it gathers force just when the conditions of its possibility seem to be about to close in on it.

Desire's Method

The madness of possibilities. But is there a method in all of this movement? Or again, you might say, why do we need a method, given at best the sociological drudgery, at worst the pseudo-scientific pretensions associated with such a term? Part of the problem is the wonderful way in which desire runs all over the place. Beyond a taxonomy of good or bad manifestations of desire, what interests me are questions about how to use queer desire in such a way that it is not condensed in an individualizing logic and measure.

Put another way, the question is how to use desire so as to put it to work as a singular and queer form of movement, so that desire points us not to a person, not to an individual, but to the movement, the different relations between various body parts: desire set off in commotion, triggered in connection with the motion of the muscles of her neck. It should be clear that I am talking about the relation of images, parts of bodies and things, not individuals.[5] This is to construct the image as having "a certain existence…situated half-way between the 'thing' and the 'representation'" (Bergson, 1990: 1). The productive force of desire can then be seen as it incessantly spins lines between the "thing" and the "representation," with desire as the force that connects or disconnects images and things. Desire "does not have, strictly speaking, an object, but merely an *essence* that spreads itself over various objects" (Deleuze, 1991: 110). Or, as Foucault calls "*la pensée-émotion,*" it is a "movement which animates the soul and propagates itself spontaneously from soul to soul…bringing forth pleasures, uneasiness, manners of seeing, sensations that I have already had or that I intuit that I must feel some day" (1994: 249; 1982: 244). And it is here that we can glimpse in action the difference of kind that queer desire seeks to relate. Far from essentializing queer desire within some individuals, this is to argue that this desire is an essence that spreads itself over things. As we catch our bodies configured on bodies, desire "communicates a kind of reminiscence, an excitement that allows [her] to follow" (Deleuze, 1990: 111).

There is no question that we are already within the engagements of desire, engaged and being engaged. And we are perhaps already beyond the interpretation of images that seeks the origin of meaning, that seeks to fix impossible equivalences, that wishes to interpret images for their authentic queerness. Rather, the task at hand is to seek out becomings, becoming-horse-becoming-lesbian. And, as is perhaps clear through the meanderings of this chapter, I use the polymorphous ways of desire in a polyvalent manner. To briefly retrace the path I have forged, this is to put desire to work in lines of flight, lines that scramble the subjective, the sexual, the social. In this framework, becoming-horse is a strategy for figuring the undoing and the redoing of the lines between and among entities. The figure of becoming thus foregrounds the positivity of desire as a social force, a line that reworks other social forces of class, gender, ethnicity, and race. As a theoretical strategy, and as a mode of cultural criticism, desire compels us to write fully of and within the milieux that give meaning to life, milieux that constitute the singularities of social life. The challenge of writing is to become what one is describing becoming. This statement in turn belies a serious commitment to the flow and flux of social and political life as it is animated by desire. In simple terms, desire is where we start from and what we go with. While this may sound very ephemeral, I'll wager that nothing could be more concrete and pressing. For, as my mother used to say, if wishes were horses, women would ride.

3

"Love in a Cold Climate"
Queer Belongings in Québec

Fragments of a Winter Landscape

The other night I dreamed that the KKK had come to get me. Dressed in cheap black suits with Michael Jackson insignia, they looked, sounded, and moved with the bravura of Thatcherite "wide boys" of the '80s. As they surrounded my apartment, they yelled at me: "*Maudite gouine*," "Fuckin' lezzie...we'll get you; die dyke."

I woke up the next day feeling rather shaky. As my particular nightmare faded, I read in the morning paper that the school buses that the local Hasidic community uses had been defaced with anti-Semitic graffiti. While one father said hopefully that "the little ones are too young to understand," these actions are a cruel mockery of a public-service announcement currently running on television: showing a newborn baby and a graveyard, the voice-over reminds us that "at these two moments it doesn't matter who our neighbors are.... Stop the Hate."

The night preceding this latest violence, Radio-Canada had aired a telefilm by the eminent Québécois filmmaker Michel Brault. Entitled "Shabat Shalom," the film replays a previous incident when the plan to build a synagogue in the posh quartier of Outremont was met with various forms of rejection. The film takes up this story but moves it out of the Montréal region and centers on a sincere white Francophone teenage boy and his crush on a black Jewish, but not orthodox, girl. In addition, the boy bonds with his Hasidic neighbors, much to the confusion of his father. Along with the obvious good intentions of Brault, the film was interesting for the way in which it contrasted representations of happy Hasidic home life with a barren image of a single-parent Québécois father. This was indeed a motherless tale of the nation.

Two days later, the subject of the KKK returned. This time, however, it was apparently responsible for graffiti written on the office door of a professor in sociology and ethnic relations at the Université Laval in Québec City. According to the radio report, along with other images of hate there was a drawing of a plane with $300 marked next to it. While it was fairly clear that this was but a shorthand version of racist "go back to where you belong" slogans, the radio host reporting on this incident had a hard time figuring out the meaning of this sign, perhaps because in our deregulated skies $300 would get you a plane ticket from Québec City to Montréal (a distance of some 300 kilometers). Or, it would get you from Montréal to Florida, where seemingly half the Québécois population hangs out in the winter.

The question of Québec leaving Canada, and indeed of *who* was Québécois, had (once again) been raised that week with Jacques Parizeau's prediction that Québec would be a sovereign state by June 25, 1994. The leader of the opposition confidently foresaw that he wouldn't need the vote of "*non souche*"[1] Québécois to bring about independence. Thus, in a year and a bit, and on the day after the holiday of Saint Jean-Baptiste, the patron saint of Québec and of Québécois nationalism, a separate state would be founded with the votes of those who counted—those whose families count back to the first French settlers.[2]

Against this image of Québécois destiny, the week had begun with a, by now, annual outrage. At least once a year, some of the newspapers in Florida publish a photograph of a "typical" Québécois tourist ("*pure laine*" but dressed in Lycra)—beer belly hanging over his bikini briefs. Not a pretty picture, *n'est-ce pas*. However, as if to reassure the rest of the world that Montréal is more than the point of departure for overweight snow-birds, the city coincidentally unveiled our new logo. In it, the "o" of Montréal is replaced with red puckered lips. In the logic of the Greater Montréal Convention and Tourism Bureau, "it figures the lips are feminine (Montréal is, after all, a lady), classy, seductive and [they] reflect the city's *joie de vivre*" (*The Montréal Gazette*, January 28, 1993). At the same time, Montréal's English-language newspaper, *The Gazette*, ran an ad which read: "As 'Montreal' as a two-cheek kiss." Replete with yet more red lips, the text continued on a distinctly deleuzian line to argue that "when it comes to charting the changes and trends that define who we are—or who we're *becoming*—you'll find all the info inside *The Gazette*."

Telling Tales

It is now over a year since I first strung those stories together, and as I sit down yet again to try to make sense of what I want to say, my words return to trouble me. Each time I revise and rewrite this essay, something gets thrown out. And yet, it is never those tales that are chopped. Part of this has to do with the fact that my argument here proceeds through a certain use of discursive debris. Thus, a few winters ago, I set out to capture a momentary sense of what it means to experience identity in Québec. My point was to use common and banal examples that randomly occur in order to write of how identity plays out in one indifferent locale. Of course, these examples passed through my body and were caught up in my desire to understand this thing called Québécitude (Québec-ness). Looking back on it now, these tales still express some of the routinely bizarre nature of identity in Québec, some of the mundane ways in which my adopted homeland garbs itself in the trappings of nation-ness, sexuality, and gender.

However, if these tenets hold true, the body across which they pass has changed. For the sentiment that first moved me to write this essay was caught up in a lingering desire to experiment with, perhaps even to prove, my belonging in Québec. I now seem to have misplaced that desire. In part this may be due to geographical meanderings: over the last year, like many an academic, I have spent time shuffling from one point to another. This moving around and talking with people blissfully ignorant of the question "What does Québec want?" has jostled my sense of belonging. Elsewhere this lack of longing to belong might not be terribly serious. However, here in Québec, identity is an institutional project, projected on the longing for an absolute origin, predicated upon the common knowledge that as a project it will fail. It is difficult to consider living here without being touched by the constant appeals to belong.

I now find myself on the other side of that longing. However, like those stories that I am unable to erase, I cannot simply put aside the question of what it means to belong in Québec just because I happen to have had a failure of desire. And if at the outset I had hoped that in the writing I would further the intricacies of my belonging in Québec, the loss of desire does not obviate the need to think through the particular piquancy of sexuality and nationality that constitute Québécois expressions of identity. For personal reasons and driven by a theoretical exigency, I need to figure the ways in which specifically Québécois representations of identity run into very singular lines of belonging. Against general notions of nations as gendered and sexualized, I raise here the ways in which national belonging is always articulated within and across history: a history of *colonialization* in white-settler countries and a theoretical and popular history of figuring nations within an established regime dependent on certain equations of gender, sexuality, and marginality. Only in making concrete the work of such discursive equivalences can we begin to consider the singularity of belonging: the modes and manners of local being called forth at any given time and in specific spaces. Only in disabling the epistemological grounding of identity can we begin to think in more quixotic and fluid terms, terms that are beyond a normative and transcendental project of collective identity—a being in belonging enmeshed within the machinic engagements of longing, again determined by historical context, yet a being, I think, capable of rearticulating itself.

The line I follow here constantly moves through what is taken as a particularly Québécois set of belongings—the imaginary possessions that are created in the name of an identity project, the belongings that a nation, a group, a people cobble together from the past and the present. The point then is to push at these belongings, such fetish-objects of identity, in order to glimpse where they break down: where identity gives way to a singularity of "being-*such*." In Agamben's words, this is to formulate "belonging itself…being-*such*, which remains constantly hidden in the condition of belonging ('there is an *x such that* it belongs to *y*') and which is in no way a real predicate, comes to light itself: The singularity exposed as such is whatever you *want*, that is, lovable" (1993: 2).

I take Agamben's argument as a challenge and as a political commitment to analyze the vehement expressions of Québécitude—a state-funded project of identity-formation distributed across individuals—to recognize the odious creases in its belongings, the way in which a set of possessions is constituted as belonging to one group (white French settler society) at the expense of others. At the same time, the challenge of such an analysis lies not in a redistribution of those belongings in such a way that all can have a piece of the national action—rather, it is in the making strange of belongings, in queering their epistemological underpinnings, that we may be able to conceive of a manner of belonging not predicated on possession.

While one must think through categories of difference in order to grasp the composition of any given identity, once we have posed those specificities we need to question the ways in which the specificities of identity come together: the conditions of their emergence and circulation, the material circumstances that manage their movement. As Christiane Frémont argues,

"If, in metaphysics, a singularity carries to infinity that which constitutes the essence of topological singularities (namely, to decide upon the nature of a globality from the point of a certain number of local events), *singularity* has to be defined as a metaphysical point that includes in itself, in the most adequate manner possible, the greatest possible number of connections… singularity presents this particularity, that within it the connection of the local and the global is the strongest but at the same time the least visible" (1991: 115–116, 119).

In this sense, I see singularity as that point of dense connections, that point that carries within it the strongest connection of the local and the global, that singularizes specificities into a momentary structure of belonging. These are not isolated moments; rather, as Deleuze argues, "singularities, in their connection with the whole, are subject to other singularities. They are affected by these other singularities; in their interaction with them, they are transformed both into structures and into other singularities" (cited in May, 1991: 29).

Dyke Dives

As an example of the dense connections that may pass unnoticed, I want to briefly tour the shifting sites of lesbian belonging in Montréal. Here "the community" is in actual fact many and is divided along linguistic lines (Anglo and Franco lesbians seem to rarely meet) as well as generational lines (the visible Franco "community" tends to be older and retains ties from a 1970s lesbian-feminist engagement, whereas the Anglos tend to be younger and more involved in American-style queer theory and politics). These vectors are in turn inhabited by actual bodies striated by lesbian heritages. For example, here some butches and femmes in their fifties had a somewhat easier time surviving the butch-femme feuds within feminism, in part because they didn't read English.

Linguistic nationalist politics habitually enter into all corners of the city, and class geography now overlaps with a gay one. Montréal is after all a city divided (or thinks of itself as such) into the more affluent and Anglo West and the traditionally working-class Francophone East. If this generalization is already disturbed by the middle-class and mainly French-speaking quartier of Outremont to the north or by the working-class and linguistically mixed quartiers to the south, as a topological statement it then breaks open on the line of the Main, Boulevard Saint Laurent, the street that comes up from the river and is scored by the marks left from its flows of immigrants: Jewish, Portuguese, Italian, Greek, Latino, Chinese. From the lower depths of the red-light district to the upper reaches of gentrification, this street has traditionally been staked as a sort of no-man's land in linguistic battles. While languages constantly shift on the Main, move two blocks east to the longest-surviving separatist lesbian bar and you will rarely find an English-speaking dyke.

But come into that bar and consider how the lines of class, generation, and state policy move and support such a statement. Take, for example, that glorious butch over there, the one who owns a Camero, the one who picked me up, happily putting my dripping bicycle into her brand-new car. Although she speaks a bit of English, she confided in me that she has never had an anglo lover. She is part of that generation of working-class Francophones who had to "speak white" in order to survive in the anglo-dominated business world. But that cute baby butch over there couldn't put a line together in English to save herself. And she doesn't have to. Born at the turn of the 1970s, she was raised with the French face-ing of Montréal ("*le visage français*") and provincial educational policies that tend to relegate learning English to the status of basket making: nice but not essential. By the same token, her sweet Italo-Québécoise girlfriend was required by law to do all of her schooling in French, and as a result, she speaks French without an accent, English to me, Italian at home, and writes strangely in all three.

Looking around this bar, I follow the very different lines of lesbian being that congregate here. While the fact that we are all speaking in French seems to give the scene a homogeneous veneer, it is impossible to give a gloss on Francophone Québécois lesbian identity. Indeed, any generality, be it about Québécois-ness or lesbianism, flounders. Her butchness is inflected as surely as her voice with an East End hardness; a history of badly paid jobs and a suspicion against "*les anglais*" lingers in her eyes as she looks at me. And what does she see? Perhaps a femme, but one that has *"la tête car-rée"* of an Anglo, the aggressiveness of class privilege, an accent not of here but vaguely foreign, put on, too fancy. At times she doesn't understand me, doesn't expect to; at times, I no longer follow.

As an ex-bartender and waitress, I have learned a lot in bars. And as I sit here musing on dyke difference, I am reminded of the two most impor- tant bar tips: one, do not ground your identity in bars; two, do not search for depth in bar talk—take it in its very *quelconque-ness*, its so-whatness. Thus instructed, I move to trace the scratched surface of belonging here. Listening to everyday expressions of Québécois identity, I am reminded of its theoretical impossibility; I am reminded that people do routinely accept it as an actuality. Thus, while it may be my experience that having *an* iden- tity is an impossible idea, it is something that nevertheless circulates as a feasible goal and increasingly as evident fact.

That identity is problematic is hardly news within theoretical circles where identity is, of course, fragmented, decentered, and all the rest. However, it seems to me that the discourse of identity as fragmented con- tinues to be abstracted from the local ground in which one lives one's pre- sumably decentered life. As I hear these accounts of fragmentation, I won- der where the author lives: Is it the pull between a necessary level of abstraction and everyday life that fragments? I wonder why there is so little discussion of how these "factors" that fragment might be embodied and how they play out in Peoria (or Bloomington or Burlington or Regina). Bluntly put, and given the intellectual hegemony of American scholarship in this area, the contemporary theoretical tenor is one of a very American "nowhereness" and "everywhereness." Against this disembodied tone, I seek out the ways in which the local, rendered as singular, can be put to work to suggest expressions other than the general.

From where I write, it is impossible to think about belonging within Québec without considering the ways in which *l'identitaire* turns on the exi- gencies of ontology and desire. Indeed, as rhizomatic images, images that continually intertwine one alongside the other, nationality and sexuality constantly rub against each other. Moreover, against a critical mode that is content to speak of "intensity" without a trace of passion, I am convinced that an argument for the singularity of belonging must pass through and across the singularized body which writes. As Deleuze says, "It is not enough...merely to think this theoretically.... Concretely, if you define bodies and thoughts as capacities for affecting and being affected, many things change" (1992: 626).

Marginalia

In Québec, identity most often rhymes with marginality. Identity here is the expression of a complex epistemology, a way of arranging things, putting in place knowledges according to geography, history, and colonization. While the term *marginal* may sound like a quaint and old-fashioned complaint, spoken with a Québécois accent it sums up an official system held in place by the knowing constructions of gender, sexuality, and race.

Along with Stephen Muecke, I would argue that "the usefulness of center-margin is coming to an end" (Muecke, 1992: 187). For Muecke, and from the Australian context in which he speaks, the constructs of center-margin "depend on notions of cultural dominance wedded to the counter-discourse of multiculturalism" (1992: 187).[3] While these discourses and counterdiscourses are also at work here, identity debates in Québec routinely use the argument that Québec is a specific culture, a "distinct society," due to the factors of language and colonization. These historical elements are then taken as proof of Québec's marginality within the Canadian and North American context. In turn, cultural representations routinely portray Québec's specificity as marginal to the majority, as peripheral to the center, as female to the male. These discursive slippages serve to displace attention to the actual lines of singularity that compose the materiality of belonging in Québec.

It has often struck me that although most of the population lives very near and has experienced real borders, "margin" and "marginality" are used first and foremost as discursive operators. I take this term from Jean Michel Berthelot (1992), who argues that certain terms act as discursive operators which chiasmatically create discursive relations other than those they seemingly represent. As such, the margin-center equation is posed as self-evident when in fact it is always getting up to other things, forging other discursive directions.

It is, of course, for specific reasons that the singular relations of difference that motivate Canadian and Québécois discourses of identity have been figured through the discursive regime of marginality and minority. A certain understanding of colonial history and geography wells up into the present, producing pride in marginality as well as fear of being isolated. An example of "geographical pride" can be heard in the way that Québécois film director Jean-Pierre Lefebvre describes the country: "two oceans, thousands of lakes, an incomparable river; four striking seasons which annually make us relive the ritual of absolute death and life" (cited in Allor, 1993).[4] On the other hand, examples of "geographic fear" have circulated widely in the debates over the Free Trade negotiations with the United States and Mexico, and in the prognostications of what will happen after Québec separates. Marginality as a discursive operator allows for dire discourses about economic isolation, refiguring the population as stranded "drawers of water and hewers of wood." If there are good reasons for feeling marginal and isolated, marginal status tends to produce automatic and exclusive, excluding, responses. Other images of geography, isolation, and marginality come to mind: one ostensibly Canadian, the other very Québécois. The first is an animated short film produced by the National Film Board of Canada that I saw many years ago. As I recall, *Cosmic Zoom* (already dating itself as very 1970s) opens with the scene of a boy in a canoe fishing on the St. Lawrence river. We "zoom" in on a mosquito on his arm and then penetrate down through his skin and into the very atoms. The camera then whizzes up and out of the boy's body, continuing until it reaches the farthest galaxies, only to turn around and descend, finishing with an aerial shot of the boy on the river. Given the National Film Board's mandate to provide Canadians with images of themselves across the entire land, the movement and the timing of this short are intriguing. While it is common to accuse our federally funded filmmakers of being boring bureaucrats, the images here can be seen as perverting the official imperative of national identity. Produced a year before the Parti Québécois came to power, *Cosmic Zoom* resolutely gives a circumscribed, local, and vertical depiction of a river that, in fact, does cross provincial borders. If the river is stopped in its natural momentum to flow over into other areas, the individual boy is shown to be nothing but atoms, atoms which in turn are shown to be nothing compared to the galaxy. As an official document, this representation foregrounds the question, "Marginal to what?" Indeed, the very terms of identity are shown to be without foundation: the mosquito is

Elspeth Probyn

just as important as the boy; the Milky Way (as yet unclaimed by any nation that we know of) is shown to be rather more grand than the variously claimed (by Québec, Ontario, Canada) St. Lawrence seaway.

My second example concerns the poet/singer/songwriter Gilles Vigneault's quasi national anthem "Mon pays ce n'est pas un pays, c'est l'hiver" ("My country is not a country, it is winter"). While Vigneault returns us to nature, he articulates a rather peculiar synecdoche. In a place where it snows for at least six months, Vigneault's phrase starkly produces the nation as a vast and presumably empty winter. Here the temporality of winter blurs the space and the time of the nation. Modern Québec is again returned to the state that Voltaire wrote off when he summed up "La Nouvelle France" as "quelques arpents de neige" ("a few acres of snow").

These examples are but small instances in a larger repertoire of cultural images that interrelate geography, land, space, and time in very affective ways. It is a current that continues in more academic considerations of the nation. As Eli Mandel argues, there is a persistent intellectual tension "between those who believe the lines of power run North and South and those who believe they run East and West...between those who say that Canada exists *because* of its geography and those who say it exists *despite* its geography" (cited in Hutcheon, 1988: 4). The classic conceptualization of this relation is to be found in the rich work of the economic historian Harold Innis.[5] Innis's central and organizing metaphors were, of course, spatial, although their logic was deeply temporal. To be rather reductive about the lengthy and detailed historical descriptions that are at the heart of Innis's oeuvre, one can say that centers and peripheries are dialectically produced through the bias of every and any communication technology. Arguing that successive technologies regulate the spatial proximities of center and margin, and hence the power of Empire, Innis nonetheless feared their consequences, writing that the "application of power to communication industries hastened the consolidation of vernaculars, the rise of nationalism, revolution, and new outbreaks of savagery in the twentieth century" (1951: 29). At the risk of annoying Innis scholars with such a simplification of his complex thought, I would argue that it is precisely possible to present Innis in a nutshell without feeling too ridiculous because his arguments seem so very evident. Evident, that is, if you think about or teach Innis's work from a Canadian standpoint (not to mention from a particular generational viewpoint).

I remember well when I first read Innis's work. It was, thankfully, before I read his vulgarizer, Marshall McLuhan. At the time I had gone from trying to pass as a real Québécois waitress to being a graduate student in an Anglo-Canadian nationalist communication studies department. I decided that I should be working on my English Canadian belongings, not a difficult feat as my maternal grandfather had done all manner of quintessentially Canadian things. These included leaving his father's bank in the East and taking the Harvest Express, a train ride that for five dollars would take you from the East to the West, letting you off along the way to be seasonally employed by farmers. Reaching the West, he then homesteaded in northern British Columbia and also helped build some of the first roads and bridges. Along the way, he served in the trenches of World War I and sustained a deep hatred of the "motherland," especially incarnated for him in the accents and demeanor of upper-class Englishmen. Among his less salubrious forms of employment was a stint in the work camps for the unemployed during the Great Depression. During his long life, he traveled along the actual lines that were creating Canada as such. I rethought my grandfather's history and his stories in the light of Innis: the production of a national entity through the colonial technologies of transport and trade, the mapping out of Canada along the route of the Canadian National Railway, a line of national identity literally built on the bodies of Native Canadians and those Chinese and Japanese workers brought over for hard labor and often left to die as the last stake was struck. The project of forging highways, again across Native land, laid claim to a will to control time and space. The creation of Empire and colony in a land that didn't want them, the intertwining of the conquest, technology, and marginal sensibility; all these historical and geographical facts and fictions are central to Innis's theories and to certain family albums. Where else but in Canada could Gordon Lightfoot sing what amounts to an innisian theme tune: "There was a time in this old land when the railroad did not run."

And Gordon Lightfoot's *Railroad Trilogy* aptly sums up that mixture of space, longing, emptiness, and pride that allows Canada to think of itself as a miraculous, marginal line stretching across "the true North strong and free" (a line that, outside of Canada, only hockey and baseball fans will recognize as part of our national anthem). The entrenchment of this image of Canada as a perilous thread running across the continent against the tenacious downward pull of the US can be glimpsed in a 1958 promotion for the national link-up of the Canadian Broadcasting Corporation. It shows a rough map of Canada, and at the top in the far North is a graphic of a family huddled in front of the television set. Below them runs the line of receivers that stakes out the 49th parallel. The text reads: "Canadians are now linked together as a family of viewers by the CBC-TV network from sea to sea. ONE FAMILY, ONE NATION" (*Maclean's Magazine*, July 5, 1958). Of course, we know that the line is a material effect of a particular set of technologies, already shifted elsewhere. And indeed, both the railway and the broadcasting lines that epitomized the illusion of Canadian unity have been deeply cut into, more or less left in tatters as a legacy of two consecutive Conservative government mandates.

Confusing as these examples are, and tempting as it is to immediately make them into some coherent shape, I need to leave them in their jumbled state. While they are usually uttered in the romantic tones of identity, they are mere examples within Québécois and Canadian regimes of identity that can be pried from humanist moorings. Posed as coterminous with certain conceptions of nation, they can, in fact, be turned so that "each line is broken, subjected to *variations of direction*, subjected to derivations" (Deleuze, 1989: 185). These lines would then attain singularity as they intersect in different ways but never through a preexisting determination. In the moments of their intersection, these lines draw out an actuality. This actuality "is not what we are, but rather what we are becoming, that which we are in the midst of becoming, which is to say, Other, our becoming-other" (Deleuze, 1989: 190–191). In this vein, the lines of Québécois and Canadian singularity that I cite may give rise to other modes of belonging: alternative national manners.

A recent episode of *Northern Exposure* (CBS, March 1, 1994) precisely plays upon the ways in which national manners of being are neither essential nor particularly nice. In it Shelley remembers that she is Canadian and decides that her newborn baby should be officially registered as Canadian. As she hums the national anthem and croons about the superiority of Canada—from the health system to the maple syrup—she is shocked to find out that the father of her child, Holling, has given up his Canadian cit-

izenship and, more specifically, his Québécois identity. "You've forgotten
the motto of Québec" she cries at him. "I remember, 'je me souviens'"—
"What do you remember, Holling?" With national pride, she leaves to visit
a friend in Canada, and filled with remorse, thinking that he will never see
Shelley or his child once they taste the delights of Canada, Holling takes
off on his snowmobile to bring them back. Both of their journeys back to
the homeland are a bit rough. Shelley finally gives up trying to buy cute
little Mountie dolls ("perfect Christmas presents"), as she cannot find a
shop assistant and when she does, the woman is indifferent, if not rude.
Holling woos Shelly back to Alaska by singing a stirring rendition of "This
land is your land, this land is my land." They then return to Alaska with a
presumably American-Canadian child, a happy outcome that recalls, even
as it twists, the 1970s "Entre Amis/Between Friends" ideology of US-
Canadian relations.

In this episode supposedly essential national characteristics—
weather, geography, history—are turned into a tale about temperament
and manners of being. An apt and timely ode to the Canadian medical system (the episode aired during the height of the fuss about the Clinton
health care plan) is tempered by representations of Canadian indifference.
The scenes of far-flung parts of Canada and the United States are linked
with a scene at the border crossing, where Holling on snowmobile comes
close to having to strip in order to produce the required wads of docu-
mentation. All the while, at the top of both nations the land is equally
bleak on both sides, the margin of one country identical to the other.

If *Northern Exposure* manages to give us two nations as merely two
manners of being a nation and neatly places the nations of Canada and
the United States within the indigenous First Nations, much of critical
writing returns us to the margin as gendered and sexualized scene. In
some cases the margin becomes the site of an obscene playing out of ethnic, gendered, and sexual difference, all conflated in the name of an
authentic being. For instance, in an early essay, Fredric Jameson writes
that "the only authentic cultural production today has seemed to be that
which can draw on the collective experience of marginal pockets of the
social life of the world system" (1979: 140). In and among Jameson's pockets one finds "black literature and blues, British working-class rock,
women's literature, gay literature and the 'roman québécois'" (1979: 140).

Elspeth Probyn

Another theorist of postmodernism, Linda Hutcheon, states that "in Canadian writing the two major (but by no means only) new forms to appear have been those that embody ethnicity and the female" (1988: 18). Coincidently, Jameson's description of an "ethnic" (the preeminent Québécois novelist Hubert Aquin) becomes strangely gendered as he describes his "writing [as] shooting (in both homicidal and sexual senses)" (1983: 223):

> What I have found…is that when this garish surface is approached ever more closely, as with the smears of an open wound, suddenly microscopic hues appear, a whole oil-slick rainbow of the most delicate and unusual subcutaneous perception, swarming, marbled…. Even the exclamations now seem to me to have an inner tension, to speak their pent-up 'emotion' with all the tautness of a drawn bow. (1983: 216)

In this passage, Jameson presents how he came to terms with what he calls Aquin's "first-person self-indulgent" voice. However, instead of being an example of the singularity of Québécois writing, Aquin is used to embody marginality. And a strange body it is: weird quasi-pornographic codes—the garish surface, the smears of an open wound, the swarming and marbled subcutaneous etc. The seemingly endless slide from lips to lips is abruptly stopped once and for all by "the tautness of a drawn bow."

While this example is perhaps overly blatant, I use it to illustrate the problems of speaking of national or ethnic identity in the singular, outside a gendered and sexualized regime of established knowledges. Too often, identity slides into difference, compulsively figured as sexual and marginal. That this is a tautological system does not impede its profusion both in popular and intellectual discourses. Banally coded in sexual terms, it becomes extremely difficult to talk of gender, nation, minority, majority, sexuality, homosocial relations, and homosexuality "at once separately *and* together" (de Lauretis, 1988: 17).

Unraveling the Romance

Singularizing this web of lines is easier said than done. Key to this knot is the historical confusion which places women as the general term of sexual difference. Without entering into a long discussion about the sex-gender system, I do want to remark on the way in which gender is generally taken as the mark of difference. Here I take from French materialist feminism,[6] which until very recently hardly mentioned the term *genre* (gender). Instead, theorists such as Christine Delphy, Nicole-Claude Mathieu, and Colette Guillaumin start from the concept of "*les rapports de sexe*" (the social relations of sex). In her early article, "Pratique du pouvoir et idée de nature" (1978), Guillaumin clearly lays out how "*les rapports de sexe*" work:

> The ideological-discursive face of the relation renders the material and appropriated entities as *things in thought itself*; the object is dismissed "out" of the social relations and inscribed within a pure materiality. By inference, the *physical* characteristics of those who are *physically* appropriated are taken as the *causes* of the domination which they suffer (1978: 6).

In Guillaumin's theory, "*le sexage*" designates the material and symbolic appropriation of one class (women) by another (men). Throughout her work in feminism and on ethnicity, Guillaumin has always refused difference even as others reproduced difference as a celebratory catch-all in feminism. For her, difference is always difference *from*, an epistemology that allows for a subjugated position created in opposition to, and producing, the general. As Guillaumin characterizes the situation,

> It is not certain that men are sexed beings; they *have* a sex, which is different. We *are* sex, in its entirety. Indeed, there isn't really a masculine (there isn't a grammatical *gender* male). One says 'masculine' because men have kept the general for themselves. In fact, there is a general and a feminine, a human and a female. (1978: 16)

Guillaumin's argument about the construction of sex classes through the constitution of the general effectively problematizes an important obstacle in thinking about the singular relations designated by the concepts of gender, sexuality, and homosociality. Her term *sexage* identifies the way in which material entities (women) are appropriated in order to allow for the construction of a general class: men. Moreover, through appropriation, women as historical individuals are thrown out of the system of social relations and are deemed to ontologically constitute the

Elspeth Probyn

"pure materiality" of nature. If Guillaumin's analysis focuses on the material constitution of a founding class, her term *sexage* describes the constitution of difference necessary to the creation of the general. Incarnated as difference, women (and more precisely, women's bodies) can be understood as the discursive operator that allows for the creation and maintenance of the same: the homosocial general. Rendered as such, as actual material entities they are dismissed from the system. Her analysis thus compels a problematization of gender in general and especially of the ways in which it is used to construct general models of society and of nation.

Turning to some common images, we can see examples of this construction of the general in action. On the one hand, Canadian images take on an ontology of gendered and heterosexual positioning: Canada as the defenceless maiden to the American hulk. In turn, in Québec these images articulate the Francophone minority as the marginal female: at different times and sometimes simultaneously she is wooed, rejected, scorned, or continually in the midst of initiating divorce. In a wonderful version of this scenario, Vigneault sings, "Tu peux ravaler ta romance" (which can be translated as "You can have your romance," or "Take your romance and shove it"). Here a woman tells her husband that she's had enough, that "his kisses lack punch" (or more literally, they "lack follow through": "*manque de suite*"). It is, of course, the "marriage" of Canada and Québec that is finally at an end.[7]

This trope of women telling their husbands to shove it continues in a short film by Michel Brault. In *La Dernière Partie* (*The Last Match*), Brault tells the story of a woman in her mid-fifties who has had it with her husband. Louise has particularly had it with their Saturday night ritual of going to the Forum to watch the Montréal hockey team, Le Canadien. Sitting in the bleachers among the roaring fans, there and then she decides to leave him. When the husband eventually realizes that Louise is gone, he goes looking for her. Again, in an explicit fashion, the question, "What does Québec want?" is made to rhyme with the infamous question, "Was will das Weib?" The answer here is told in Québécois tones as it is shown that Canada can't even adequately describe its long-standing partner. "Uh, she has brown eyes," says the husband to the waitress. "So do a lot of wives," she replies. When he does find her, Louise calmly tells him that she is going, that she has had enough of hockey night (in Canada), that she no longer can stand the way he makes love to her, that she gets through it by staring at a line in the ceiling. With that, she walks out through a turnstile and the screen fades to white.

The gendering of Québec and Canada as a couple in the throes of divorce is by now so common that it needs little explanation. It comes as no surprise that once again Québec is posed as marginal to and different from Canada and that this difference is then embodied in the wife. What is interesting, however, is the way in which these images produced by two middle-aged men so strongly identify with the woman's point of view. In both Vigneault's song and Brault's film, we see from the eyes of the women, women trapped in unsatisfactory relationships, women who are not getting enough good sex for it to be worth it. And in neither of these cases is the wife represented as thinking of another man; staring at the cracked line in the ceiling, she just desperately wants out of an unfulfilling arrangement. To further complicate things, the French "minority" makes up, in actual fact, 82 percent of the population within Québec, which then allows some Anglophone-rights groups to position themselves as marginal and in need of protection. This then produces a discourse of Anglophones as "emasculated" in relation to the Québécois strongman. Given the historical relations, this produces a discursive structure of male to male, homosocial bickering. And how better to depict this relation than through images of Le Canadien's players (a team more familiarly known in English as the "Habs," a shortened form of the pejorative term *les habitants*, images of graceful and violent male bodies on the rink, cheered on by those less so in the stands?

Familiar as these images are, they also begin to suggest that the general troping of national identity as gendered and heterosexualized is in the midst of cracking up into lines that have no necessary direction. It seems that the unraveling of identity brings on an orgy of remembering and forgetting. In the heat of this moment, I turn to even more banal images that remember to forget and forget to remember. I turn on the television and feel the impact of the communal amnesia and remembrance generated in the gendering of the Québécois nation. The most striking of these images emanate from Québécois *téléromans*, a genre which in Québec resolutely turns to the past. "Here, matter (which is image-movement) changes into memory (thus, into image-time), and the present, never identical to itself, is doubled with the virtual image of the past it will become" (Ropars-Wuilleumier, 1988: 121).

For the sheer numbers who loyally watched it, the dramatic television series *Les filles de Caleb* is an obvious place to start.[8] It is a fairly straightforward tale centered around two of my favorite figures: the schoolmarm, and horses. Set at the turn of the century, the protagonist, Emilie, is the eldest daughter of a large family who has to fight her father to continue her studies. She becomes the sole teacher in a one-room school until she unfortunately falls in love with one of her students. There then follows a rather stereotypical tale of marriage, hardship, and heartbreak as her increasingly sodden husband takes off for the woods, leaving Emilie to bear and raise something like ten children. The tentatively happy ending has Emilie finally leaving the drunken and debt-ridden husband.[9]

Summarized in this way, *Les filles de Caleb* sounds like any number of mawkish historical dramas. Indeed, on a general level, the story of a young, attractive, and independent woman teacher who tames her male charges has been played out in any number of locales. Notably, though perhaps not surprisingly, if one thinks of examples as heterogenous as *The King and I*; *The Prime of Miss Jean Brodie*; *Sarah, Plain and Tall*; *My Brilliant Career*; *Anne of Green Gables*; or the recent television program *Dr. Quinn, Medicine Woman* (which *TV Times* heralded as the "flowering of the frontier"), these tales are often set in outposts of nations. The woman battles both geographic and masculine odds in order to bring about civilization, and closure is assured by overcoding one individual man as the quintessential summation of roughness, wildness, and nation-ness who falls in love with her. An interesting twist to this heterosexualization of the homosocial frontier can be seen in *Northern Exposure*'s narrative about the founding and civilizing of Cicely, Alaska, by a lesbian couple. And in Muriel Spark's *The Prime of Miss Jean Brodie* (1961), it is, of course, "my gels" that are the focus of Miss Jean Brodie's attentions in a Scotland very much on the border of Englishness.

If in many ways *Les filles de Caleb* seems to resemble any national telling of the historical frontier tale, it is nonetheless told in local and excessive tones. One of the more memorable scenes takes place before Emilie's marriage to Ovila. The two men, father and future husband, bond as Ovila brings his stallion to the farm of Emilie's parents in order to mate it with the father's new mare. (Horses run through this story from the begin-

ning: the first episode has Emilie rebelling against the double standard of
work that the girl children have to carry. Caleb is particularly harsh on
Emilie in return, and we are given to understand that his treatment of her
is due to his distress from having to put down his favorite horse.)

But back to the mating scene. As the stallion begins to mount the
mare, Caleb instructs his wife to cover the eyes of the younger children
and to send them away. Emilie and Ovila, however, are placed to look on
(and to be looked at) as the impossibly proud father orchestrates the mating. In a long series of parallel close-up shots, we see the horse penis pene-
trating the mare as Ovila nuzzles Emilie from behind. Shot for shot, the
penis of the horse segues into shots of Emilie in ecstasy. The lengthy back-
and-forth movement is accompanied by soundtrack music but no dia-
logue. Finally the sexual tension is broken when Emilie's sister (who is destined to become a nun) enters the scene and they all nervously giggle.

Needless to say, this scene (which aired at eight in the evening on
Radio Canada—the state Francophone television network) caused snig-
gers and giggles elsewhere. The best spoof was on *Bye, Bye 91*—an end-of-
the-year satiric program—when the well-known actress Dominique
Michel played Emilie. In a re-creation of the schoolroom, Michel rips off
her stays and begs Ovila to "do like the horses." At which Ovila, played as
the village fool, stands up and whinnies and prances. This really very silly
parody is in many ways more interesting than the original. For a start, the
original almost too blatantly insists on the lines of equivalence between
humans and horses. When *Les filles de Caleb* was dubbed in English and
played on the CBC (for adult audiences at ten o'clock at night), the actress
who plays Emilie (Marina Orsini) said in a radio interview that the point
was that "we wanted to show that sex between animals and between
humans is beautiful and natural."

While Orsini presumably was not advocating interspecies sex, her
words echo the seemingly inevitable correspondence of the mare and
Emilie. In the guise of a natural flow, the independent schoolmistress is
brought into line with the mare. Following Guillaumin's argument, this is
a very telling instance of woman dismissed from the ideological-discursive
realm of the social in order to become inscribed within the "pure materiality" of nature. As her body is appropriated for the construction of a discourse on the nation, she becomes reproduction, pure and simple. And as

such, she performs a "misrecognized relation" between animal husbandry and the management of the nation. In turn, the exigency of mating is felt and is caught up with the incessant reminders white Québécoise women must reproduce in order for the nation to survive.

The Bedroom of the Nation[10]

If *Les filles de Caleb* presents us with these lines of equivalence, these relations of the same, it does so perilously. This is precisely why I like the spoof more than the actual scene it sends up. While it is but one incidental moment, it nonetheless speaks of alternative relations of belonging as it scrambles and frees up lines of identity. Beyond the pious words of Orsini, this version plays identity at the edge. Yes, it says, Québec has historically been fucked by Canada. However that oft-repeated line is now eroticized, and the tired metaphors of domination, nature, marginal, feminine, and masculine are placed so that they threaten to fall into literalized desire. And as Emilie commands sex, the husband is shown up as incompetent and impotent. While Québec may still be represented in the guise of womanhood, she is now a fully and wildly desiring being who may just take her pleasures elsewhere, anywhere.

In other words, if *Les filles de Caleb* is interesting as an event (with its spinoffs and spoofs, its connections and reconnections), it is because the nation as the manifestation of heterosexuality is posited as teetering among various orders of specificities: from the fictional genre that is translated into the Québécois form of the *téléroman* to its portrayal of romance and wilderness and its use of the figure of the schoolmarm. From sets of specificities (historical, geographical, televisual) it articulates a certain singularity of sexuality and belonging in Québec: a line that promises other manners of becoming Québécois, a manner of being that takes pleasure in queering the traditional modes of figuring identity.

But as I say this, I know that the singularity of that line of belonging only exists as one possible articulation created out of and within the materiality of the countless strata of historical narratives of identity. In short, it is a singularity that for the moment exists ambiguously within and alongside a generalized history. For a start, Québécois marginality has been expressly pronounced as analogous to other sites of oppression. For instance, marginality is spoken of in terms of "les nègres blancs d'Amérique," a phrase from the early '70s (Vallières, 1968) now making a comeback in the latest round of nationalism, a phrase that does considerable violence to the specificities of Québec nationalism and to those of the African-American civil rights movement. In addition, it is commonplace in Québec to talk of the role of the matriarch as the guardian of traditional values. In a place where strict and practiced Catholicism is just two decades down the road, in a space where steeples orient and church bells ring out (and are caught on people's answering machines), there is still a raw memory of when "les Québécoises" were to build the nation through reproduction. However, if this is common to many articulations of Catholicism and national projects, in Québec it was, and continues to be, connected to, and rerouted, by the virtual absence of men. As televisual images compulsively return to the past, we are given an account of the spatial configurations of early Québécois nationhood that places men in a space-off; a telling of the past wherein men just were not very important—to women or to the national project. A strangely empty space, peopled by women and priests, it is a temporality predicated on a gendered geography of women securing the nation just as some of the First Nations were used by the government, physically uprooted in order to safeguard the North. It is indeed my country as winter, not as actual land, an arrangement ordered by priests instructing the women to perform the "revenge of the cradle," the clergical dictate to populate a religiously Francophone nation. In *Les filles de Caleb*, Emilie gives birth in every second episode, and she has a penchant for doing it outside in the snow. As she bears the nation in the elements, the husband is elsewhere.

In two other recent television dramas, the matriarch moves to the city. In *Montréal ville ouverte* and in *Montréal, P.Q.*, the history of Montréal in the '40s is told through and around the figure of the matriarch as bordello owner. Here she is the figure of mediation between Anglophone vice (in *Ville ouverte* all the "baddies" speak English or heavily accented French) and the clergy.[11] For the most part, the madams are sympathetic and, in an interesting twist on an old tale, they are maternal to their charges at the same time as they hold dear the pleasures of hot sex. As an Italian madam reminisces, "All those young bodies, I feel them and I have the 'chair de poule'" ("goosebumps"). Once again "true" Québécois men are elsewhere. The only ones who remain are the priests, those "men in dresses," and homosexuals.[12]

If the general articulation of gender and nation holds, the singular conditions of its possibility shift its sense. Rather than posing the nation as female, as minority is to majority, the Québécois nation is both produced and displaced as female through images of the matriarch. The discursive operator here is indeed "woman," but she instigates movement between the matriarch and women, with Québécois men being displaced from the system. If the nation is gendered, it is through the relations of sex, the social and discursive work involved in constructing relations between women and the matriarch as guardian of the nation. Alongside the general understanding of the nation as positioned within and produced out of a heterosexualized play of minority-majority relations, the local and singular images here are of the matriarch winking at the absence of men. Again, this is banal, common knowledge, and as the noted playwright Michel Tremblay replied when he was asked why there were no male characters in his plays: "Because there *are* no men in Québec" (cited in Schwartzwald, 1991: 180).

This spatial arrangement then upsets any general argument about the nation as gendered as feminine within a heterosexual contract. Just as the discursive movement that allows for the nation as gendered is between women with men as the outside term, the sexualization of the Québécois nation has traditionally been expressed through the example of the homosexual man. As Robert Schwartzwald argues[13], this is a common thread within Québécois discursive relations of nation-ness: "In popular culture, homosexuality has served as an accepted metaphor for national oppression and continues to do so" (1991: 180). In Guy Ménard's terms, the images of Québec national identity and contemporary gay affirmation are so closely intertwined that the failure of the 1981 referendum on sovereignty becomes "a failed coming-out" (1983: 331). The figure of the homosexual man then further displaces any general relation of nation and heterosexuality. The relations of difference here are not those of female to male, minority to majority, but rather of male homosexuality to national homosociality, which is to say of minoritized men to the majority.

A striking example of this relation is clearly illustrated in one of the highest-grossing Québécois films, *Le Déclin de l'empire américain*. While the director, Denys Arcand, has built his entire filmic oeuvre on images of the nation (from his early documentaries *Nous sommes au coton* and *Le confort et l'indifférence* to his recent feature-length film *Jésus de Montréal*), *Le Déclin* is a particularly striking construction of the Québécois nation through homosocial and homosexual relations. The nation is here literally produced out of the talk of university professors. But rather than talking heads, we have the female professors working out in the gym as they graphically discuss sex: s/m sex, motorbikes and sex, sex with women, sex with men, the general lack of interesting men.[14] Meanwhile, the men (their friends, lovers, husbands) are preparing dinner and enviously talking about the gay character's freedom of sexual movement. Here, as the empire supposedly falls apart around them, the nation emerges through the discursive operator of the gay man (the only one to have good sex) amidst the separate movements of male and female homosociality. It is a nicely ambiguous situation that Arcand then seems obliged to stabilize by showing the gay character pissing blood.

This scenario comes to us from the director who as early as 1964 complained about the prevalence of images of homosexual men in Québécois cinema.[15] Equating heterosexual sexual liberation with national liberty, Arcand argued that only when

> filmmakers will have forgotten their mamas so they can confidently undress the girl next door whose name is Yvette Tremblay or Yolande Beauchemin, in the full light of day...can [we] think, like Jean Renoir, about having a cinema that is free and at the same time fiercely national. A cinema of joy and conquest. (cited in Schwartzwald, 183)[16]

While contemporary Québec cinema seems to be full of undressed Yolandes and Yvettes, recently on television they seem to seriously be thinking about undressing each other. If, as Schwartzwald argues, the homosexual male is figured as the point of tension between two regimes of identity, one federal, the other provincial, a recent episode of a rather bizarre Québécois talkshow puts lesbians back in that bastion of Québécitude—the family. The talkshow in question, *Parler pour parler*, is in itself an extraordinary manifestation of Québec identity gone wild. Every Saturday the host, Janette Bertrand, focuses on a topic and invites her guests (a mixture of the usual experts and experiential bodies) to dinner. They then talk about various "taboo" subjects as they eat and drink. "La bonne," the faithful retainer, serves real food and wine and interrupts if things get too hot—or to signal to us at home that the conversation is getting hot.[17]

So it was that one Saturday night, Janette had five lesbians to dinner. Before they all sat down, we were warmed up by a lengthy dramatization entitled *L'Amour avec un grand A* ("Love with a capital L"). The drama focused on a young woman coming out to both her parents. However, the *mise-en-scène* firmly puts the focus of attention on the mother. It opens with her unable to sleep due to her intuition that one of her offspring is in trouble. And sure enough, the dyke daughter is shown in tears in her lonely apartment. Maman drags Papa out of bed and they go off to Montréal in search of the daughter. After the shock, horror, of "I am—You are?" the drama focuses on finding the daughter's missing lover. Suffice it to say that all ends well, with Maman having found the lover for her daughter. Along the way we have a very vaselined love scene between the two (it's on the camera lens), and the final images are of Maman and Papa happily back in their bed (filmed *sans* vaseline).

If this all sounds a bit corny, it's because it was. Despite, or rather because of, its ham-handedness, it is impossible to ignore the import of this drama: structurally, lesbians are being placed back inside the mainstay of Québec identity. Bookended by Maman et Papa in bed, a lesbian *couple* are enfolded, are shown as quite rightfully belonging in the otherwise traditional family. While elsewhere this might sound like mere assimilation, the family in Francophone Québec is understood and lived as a public institution as well as a private possession. The Québécois family is used to being understood as weird (being put down for its numerous offspring by Anglo non-Catholics) and cognizant of its role as a line of defense against cultural assimilation. Again, its form emerges from the history of its production through the Church as a means of creating a Francophone identity.

As opposed to the Protestant American ideal, the family is not lived or imagined here as the bastion of private individualism, and hence it cannot be as easily mobilized as the first and last line in right-wing morality. This is not to say that Québec is immune from the resurgence of so-called family values; rather, it is to say that *Parler pour parler*'s presentation of lesbians within the family works to queer the line between public belongings and private belonging. These images establish as quite legitimate the longing of the mother to have her daughter happy with the woman of her choice, the longing of daughter for acceptance without assimilation. It showcases the family as a queer site of national identity policies and history and as the space where, if we so desire, queers can and do belong.

Thus, alongside the apparent universality of the nation as imagined through the figure of the female, of the familial heterosexual fictions of nation, what we find, in fact, are lines of becoming between women and women, women and the matriarch, women and the nation, mothers and their lesbian daughters, homosexual men and priests. Lest this sound like an Edenic situation, let me be very clear that what I have described here are but fragments that have no inherent meaning. Some are historical lines that have the potential to veer into virtual relations of belonging; some serve as actual barriers to imagination. At present they are underpinned by a regime of knowledges and of knowing that turns on certain articulations of authentic being, of a nostalgic attachment to marginality, of persistent and sometimes misogynist and heterosexist inscriptions of gender and sex-uality—in short, a legitimized imaginary that revolves around *"la souche"* (the source) as possessed by right, by nature, by white males. And while other images do indeed proliferate, this obsession with the source continu-ally threatens to asphyxiate their movement.

So What?

The mere thought of this *"souche"* attenuates my desire to belong. But I return to the doubled challenge I put to myself at the beginning of this chapter. At one level, I attempt to explore some of the ways in which identity is lived out as singular manners; on another, I want to put these lines of becoming into flight by upsetting their epistemology and their ref-erence, indeed, their grounding, in a past that is continually made over and made up.

The tales with which I opened return. While you have no way of knowing whether I actually did dream up the KKK as Michael Jackson, you could verify the news stories, you could come and live Montréal (as in the French, *"j'habite Montréal"*), pass under the banner of the red lips, consult your *Women Going Places* to find the address of that dyke dive. And just up along St-Denis, you could go into a video shop and pick up copies of *Les filles de Caleb* and watch all twenty episodes interspersed with the Brault films. In other words, you too could pick up on *a* québécois manner of being, even if becoming-Québécois would be a longer and more difficult achievement. The body here, my body, is merely another being-such which trains lines of belonging as manners of being. This very so-what body cannot be privileged; its situated location is, I think, an ethical requirement in figuring the politics of a "so-what" singularity.

In turn, this brings me back to my own questions about belonging in Québec, to questions about a failure of desire. But desire is not a personal possession, so that even when personally misplaced, it continues its required work. And in fact, in working through and along the lines, I find myself pushed at by desire—as when one thinks desire spent, a certain scent can renew the sensation. And just as this is far from a general rule, so too does the desire to belong reconnect only in contact with certain singularities.

What I have tried to sketch here is an ethical practice of belonging and a politics of singularity that must start from where one is—brutally and immediately from one's belonging, modes of being, and longing. If I have insisted on the necessity of disengaging the couplings of gender, sexuality, and nation in Québécois regimes of national identity, it is because condensing these movements undoes the possibility of other manners of being and becoming, denies their present virtuality that persists in common places. The temptation to slide these terms together, to rest at the level of the general, is understandable. It is also not enough if I am to understand the full force of the images I cite.

Against understanding everyday images as somehow linked to an underlying unity, we must let them stand in their absolute "so-whatness." These examples: a dream, a civic slogan, a photograph, a film, a *téléroman*, etc., must stand alone. Not one of them is representative of "Québécoisness." However, as images which intertwine alongside each other, they hit me, they move me. And let us be clear that to speak of these images in terms of their "so-what" singularity is not to condone their violence; it is not to be blasé in the face of the terror that they may bring. Rather, in refusing the equivalence of the general, it is to be moved, to be touched by the impact of this image, and this one, and this one. It is to be bodily caught up in ways of being a being-such, a being shorn of the trammels of identity as individual possession. And if I have insisted on the work of certain discursive operators, notably those of "minority," "majority," "marginality," it is to argue that too often they are put in the service of maintaining a general order—the ordering of the same. As they graft certain relations of gender and sexuality, they participate in the reproduction of homosocial relations, of the nation as normal.[18]

Against generalized nationalist identity, it seems to me that we already see some of the singular strands of a more ethical being-such in the present images and relations all around us. It is from within these lines, away from any general picture, that we may be able to catch the construction of alternative manners, emerging singularities of belonging. Looking out of windows, walking down the street, *flâning* in the precarious sun of early spring, cruising in dives, we may glimpse alternative national manners of being, catch our bodies striving for other relations of belonging; "They rise up for a moment, and it is that moment that is important, that is the opportunity that one must grab" (Deleuze, 1990: 107).

Last night it snowed again. White upon white, upon winter-white, upon gray, upon half-white, Montréal is rendered seemingly still. But beyond the nostalgia of past picture cards, people's paths criss-cross in unexpected ways. When we are brought together momentarily by the impasse of a wall of snow, she smiles uncertainly: "Enough snow for you?" While it's hardly poetic, while the sight is not really majestic, it may be the start of something or nothing at all; it is a very small gesture of being, if not loving, in a cold climate.[19]

4

Suspended Beginnings
Of Childhood and Nostalgia

Childhood as Event

I am sometimes baffled when people whom I have only just met remark
on the fact that I grew up in Wales. I am momentarily embarrassed by the
thought that in published work I've made a big deal over something small:
growing up. If within cultural studies, feminism, and gay and lesbian writing returning to childhood is not uncommon, it can, as I have found out,
return to haunt. It is also a paradoxical turn; in my case I use the phrase "I
grew up in Wales" as both a short form to explain the quirks of my accent
and, more importantly, to try to indicate some of the backward-and-for-
wardness and the straying of any identity. But, of course, once said, it stations one, places one in relation to something that can take on the weight
of origin: that's where you're from, that's why I'm like that, that explains
it, etc.

In this chapter, I want to examine some of the ways that childhood is
produced as a sustained mode, indeed as a structure of feeling, within some
gay and lesbian fiction. As the Belgian writer Amélie Nothomb puts it in
her novel about childhood and the desire of one girl for another: "Quand je
serai grand, je penserai à quand j'étais petit" ("When I'll be big, I'll think
about when I was small"). Her words can be used to sum up a pronounced
trend within gay and lesbian fiction, a line that winds around a return to
childhood. While in Nothomb's tale, *Le sabotage amoureux* (1993), childhood is
presented as sufficient unto itself—the narrator and the narrative mode
are captured within being-child; indeed, childhood *is* being itself ("être
enfant, c'est-à-dire être" [83])—in Anglo-American circles a generation of
grownups are thinking out loud about when they were small. This is not
an especially gay and lesbian phenomenon; nonetheless, there are good
reasons to consider the specificities of the queer turn to childhood. In this
vein, I want to consider gay and lesbian childhood as event: a tangled discursive skein, a multilevel production in which strata of truth, representation, history, science, and experience compete.

For Foucault, as for Deleuze, events oppose essence, or rather
attempts to produce essence are already contained within "the event." In

his 1977 review of Deleuze's *Loqique du sens*, Foucault connects event and phantasm in ways that seem especially relevant to thinking about childhood:

> The event (assimilated in a concept, from which we vainly attempted to extract it in the form of a fact, verifying a proposition, of *actual experience*, a modality of the subject, of concreteness, the empirical content of history); and the phantasm (reduced in the name of reality and situated at the extremity, the pathological pole, of a normatizing sequence: perception-image-memory-illusion). (1977: 180)

Considering childhood in these terms, as event, thus turns our attention to the ground upon which several orders of things are ranged: on the one hand, historical facts, scientific propositions, empirical observations, actual experiences, and attempts to render them concrete; on the other hand, phantasmatic features of childhood, images that carry childhood into the realm of the pathologizable, images that float as memory (which are, of course, incorporated as fact, proposition, observation, and experience). Any critical interest in current constructions of queer childhood as event must therefore take into account a heterogeneous ensemble of statements: moral panics about gays and lesbians having children; the American Psychiatric Association's pathologizing of childhood gender identity; childhood as the structuring *modus operandi* in gay and lesbian writing. Moreover, childhood as event requires that attention be paid to the modes in which it is articulated: as originary, as nostalgic, as quintessential, as anecdotal, as fiction, as fact.

Against a trend to posit childhood as a point of departure in the construction of queer being, a maneuver which indicates a barely hidden yearning within some formations of identity politics for something that would ground difference ineluctably, I want to consider childhood as the point from which we "laugh at the solemnities of origin." With the Nietzschean glee Foucault evokes in his discussion of genealogy, I want to place childhood on the surface, to refuse it the anterior status of guarantee. Rather than seeing in childhood a common point of queerness, a garden of Eden from which we all fled or were expelled only to return ever after in nostalgic wonderment and wandering, I would have queer theory use childhood "to record the singularity of events outside of any monstrous finality" (Foucault, 1977: 139). The lofty origin then becomes no more than "a metaphysical extension which arises from the belief that things are most precious and essential at the moment of birth" (Foucault, 1977: 143).

To laugh at childhood as the origin of whatever is, I think, a necessary move in realizing the seriousness of the political possibilities of queer childhood. But politicizing childhood must proceed by making birth and childhood into a question of "so-what" or "whatever"; they must be pried from their position as individualized and precious possessions. In other words, far from treating childhood as an originary moment from which we might emerge as proud grownup queers, we need to remake childhood into evidence of the necessary absence of any primary ground in queer politics.

It is in this sense that I read a recent novel by Dale Peck. In *Martin and John* (1993), a tale is structured through stories of love and loss in the time of AIDS: two characters, two childhood friends, two lovers, caught up within several different but coexisting time periods. While the scenarios change the names remain the same, creating a movement of repetition and difference held together by a line of memory that recoils from the end. Far from memorializing childhood as monument, Peck clearly positions it as a basis that does not exist. Summed up in the line, "this is not the worst thing I remember" (5), childhood is and is not. As a structuring device, the phrase "this is not the worst thing I remember" is seldom spoken but nonetheless serves to hold childhood and gay love together. If the boy's memories of being ashamed of his mother's shame of her queer child are recounted as "this is not the worst thing I remember," the second and last time we read the phrase is at the end of the novel, after his lover Martin has died of AIDS: "I wrote: this is not the worst thing I remember, and then, I don't know why, but I wrote something that hadn't happened" (225).

With this simple line and elegant strategy, Peck manages to rewind the story he has told, a tale of memory and forgetting, of remembering but holding back against the one thing that would be the worst, the one thing that would forever anchor the meaning of life itself. Rather, as he writes:

> Memory is my only possession, but it resists ownership. I remember the first thing I wrote: this is the worst thing I remember, I wrote, and then I stopped writing. Nothing came after that sentence; nothing ever did. Nothing announced itself as the worst of it all, although many, many things— images, sounds, sensations, sentences even, though I don't remember who first wrote or spoke them—all vied for the honor. (225)

This is not the worst thing I remember, this is not the worst thing I remember—the phrase easily slips into mantra. As such, as an instrument for thought, it both conjures and controls the past, or tries to. But if this is not the worst thing, if the worst thing can't be said or known, touched or held in place, then the worst thing can't ever really be past. Childhood past is thus refused any status as an ordering point of departure in a teleology of origins.

A line wrought out of childhood experience, the phrase sums up how I feel about my own childhood: it is not the worst thing I remember; I don't remember it; it hovers there as a horizon constantly receding before me, rubbed out in my inability to remember, caught in the knowledge that I must have had one. Luckily, my sister had one close to mine and remembers. Indeed, perhaps I don't have to remember, as I can rely on her uncanny ability to recollect our joined childhoods. As she charts the duration and arrangement of our various childhood displacements, I see the past through her eyes, literally through an image I have of a photograph of her taken by our older brother when she was six or seven. The photo, which is slightly Arbus-esque, shows her looking straight at the camera with the candor of someone who has already seen too much but continues to regard and record. So vivid was her recall at times that I could have sworn that she was making it up. Of course, this is now theoretically familiar—that the past is made up, fictions of the past, the past as fiction.

I raise this not as evidence but as a shortcut, a path hastily cleared leading from childhood to memory, and thence to the spaces and ways in which memory may proceed. For against the idea that childhood is a private entity, what is striking is the way in which childhood is at once the most personal of possessions and the most public of concerns. It is also, increasingly, something that you may have foisted upon you, either your own or those of others. Both personal and public, childhood is a staple of the coming-out story, a point at which many recollect the realization of their queerness. Individual and common, story after story recounts the feeling of somehow not belonging, of not fitting in, until the move is made to belong to another community and another kind of family.

But we also need to ask, to whom does childhood belong? In disciplinary terms, childhood—childhood and sexuality, or the childhood of gays and lesbians—is the possession of several fields, notably psychology, psychiatry, and psychoanalysis. Politically, the right in several countries has tried to ensure that childhood belongs to it as a "motherhood" issue, and, indeed, in many key areas children's rights have supplanted those of their mothers.

The problematic arising from these contestations is a more general one concerning the use of childhood. I return again to the necessity of conceiving childhood as event—event placed on the *outside*. For if we are to remake childhood as a political tactic to be used to turn identity inside out, we need to deploy the historicity of childhood as event: childhood memories; childhood as a set of possessions we carry with us; childhood as a designated point of departure; childhood as the source of public pathologization (the beginning of the "problem" of homosexuality); childhood as an epistemology of origins. This then begs the questions of how and whether gay and lesbian childhoods are different. Nowadays, it seems hard to find anyone who actually had a normal, happy childhood. (Of course, the terms *normal* and *happy* are already under erasure and are in any case not coterminous.) Unhappy childhood memories, moreover, seem to be infectious, with one person's story spurring another's. And while this may set up lines of connection, it may also turn into a dreary game of matching pain and unhappiness, a grim contest which quickly dissolves any autonomous status that these stories, experiences, and their conditions of possibility—their status as event—may possess.

Such matching then gets in the way of rendering these experiences singular. For instance, a passage from Edmund White's brilliant novel *A Boy's Own Story* (1982) immediately brought to mind a similar story from my own childhood. In White's story, the father presents the narrator's sister with "a 'life bill', the itemized expenses he'd incurred in raising her over twenty-one years, a huge sum that was intended to discourage her from thoughtlessly spawning children of her own" (38). Reading White, I was "driven" to write the following: "In the dearth of memories, I come across a phrase, the one constant that I remember from my childhood was the oft-repeated statement that we were spoiled. The cost of childhood was registered. Instead of sex education, we repeatedly had lessons on the economic facts of life."

Now, while there is a certain resemblance, there are several important distinctions. White's story is in a novel that may be in part autobiographical but nonetheless is a story told by a gifted novelist. It is also a tale of a young boy realizing his gayness; the anecdote about his sister serves to further the presentation of this childhood recognition. On reflection, there is nothing but difference here. In addition to the important fact that one is fiction and the other something I "made up," the economic, class, gender, and geographical distances should mark the specificities involved in each narrative. The only thing that could be said to be the same is that White's character grows up gay and that I turn out lesbian, which is to say that there is really very little in common. That I may enjoy White's writing and be inspired by it is one thing; quite another, and where for me the problem arises, is that the rush for commonality ("our queerness") collapses completely different orders.

For my central concern is not childhood *per se* but rather the deployment of childhood: how to write childhood, and, if that writing is fictional, how to place it with other sets of writing childhood (be it scientific, historical, empirical, or theoretical texts), how to maintain the singularities of childhood experience. While childhood may form a common pool of traits (and this is debatable), what I want to avoid is a swapping of memories, a textual game of "Oh, that happened to me too." In short, I want a strategy for mining the richness of childhood, a tone of writing that encourages a diverse exploitation of childhood with an eye to present exigencies. I want a tactic that enables certain formulations of belonging but disables general statements about identity that would ultimately stall the singular force of queer interventions.

Because of all this and more, I begin with Sedgwick's insight that "the very word 'queer' embraces, instead of repudiating, what have for many of us been formative childhood experiences of difference and stigmatization" (1993: 157). But while I fundamentally agree with Sedgwick, I also want to linger over the ways in which we do indeed embrace those experiences, to ask what we may do with them. For while queer children are undoubtedly informed by difference, I am loath to posit this abstracted difference as the foundation from which queer theory might unproblematically proceed. And perhaps due to my "high Church" background, the verb *to stigmatize* carries for me the sense of stigmata. (In my childhood phase of wanting to become a nun, I remember preparing for the moment they would appear by burning the middle of my palms with the car cigarette lighter, which made beautifully circular wounds.) Of course, we can suspend the notion of stigmata as evidence of origins in favor of the idea that "the body manifests the stigmata of past experience and also gives rise to desires, failings and errors" (Foucault, 1977: 148). However, if we are to use childhood as stigmata to be studied on the present body, we must treat that body not as individual, possessed of and as truth, but as "the inscribed surface of events…the locus of a dissociated Self…and a volume in perpetual disintegration" (Foucault, 1977: 148).

As Agamben argues in *Enfance et histoire*, childhood "cannot simply be something that proceeds chronologically" (1989: 62); "we must renounce nothing less than this concept of origins founded on a model that the natural sciences have themselves abandoned and which defines origin as a point in a chronology, as an initial cause which separates in time a before self from an after self" (1989: 64). Rather than positing childhood as some self-evident ground from which we may unhesitatingly speak, I take from Agamben the challenge of "effectuating an *experimentum linguae*, thus to risk oneself in a perfectly empty dimension…where one finds oneself faced with the pure exteriority of language" (1989: 11).

Here my experiment involves thinking about childhood memories within an "empty dimension." In other words, they are beginnings that are constantly wiped out, forcing me to begin again and again. This is the ethical project that Agamben designates as "la tâche enfantine," "the childish task of the next generations" (1989: 15). For me, this also entails a radically interdisciplinary mode. The task, in other words, is to place childhood on the outside of several disciplinary endeavors. For if I am struck by the conspicuous thematization of childhood within gay and lesbian fiction, I cannot ignore the ways in which childhood is mobilized by other disciplines that are as diverse as political theory and cognitive psychology. This then requires careful thinking about the articulations of fiction and empiricism, autobiography and cultural theory, history and stories.

In this rethinking, I turn to Foucault's writing on fiction. As Jacques Revel states, "At the very least since Freud, we know that fiction, just like history, is a system of intelligibility" (cited in Bellour, 1989: 172). As such, as a system that organizes statements, producing the conditions of possibility for others, fiction is, for Foucault, already on the outside. As he writes, "The fictive is precisely that which is neither above nor [held within as] the intimate secret of the quotidian, but this trajectory of an arrow which strikes us and offers us all that which appears [all that is there]" (1994: 280). At least two things are clear here: that, for Foucault, it is the doubled movement of the line of the social that fiction traces and allows us to grasp. Fiction "raises up not that which is past so that its effect might return to the present, but rather it [raises] that which is in the midst of happening" (cited in Bellour, 1989: 176). In keeping with his insistence on the work of the double, fiction is to be situated among other social operations as a technology of the self: the "singular wrinkles" of a sentence, a modality of bending and pleating the line of the social in the service of constituting the social. Or, as Raymond Bellour puts it, "This affectivity...this is fiction itself as the operation of reality, affirming itself as the only reality possible.... It is both the law of composition and organization, and an ethic for the invention of the self" (in Bellour, 1989: 177).

Fiction for Foucault is caught up in mechanisms of distance, proximity, and space. It is that space between *les mots et les choses*, that distance between words and memories, that gap between things and our names. It is, of course, a distance inherent in language, indeed, "the fictive is the distancing proper to language" (Foucault, 1994: 280). It is one of the principles in the dispersion of things on the surface of the social that breaks with any linear and causal model of the association of the words and things, statements, and their positivity. "It is a vertical or arborescent relation that...holds figures ['as if suspended'] which, instead of being ordered by time, distribute themselves along different rules" (1994: 282). For the purposes of my argument, Foucault's use of fiction reorders thinking about the relation of writing to memory, of writing experience to self. Simply put, it disorders any search for origin, any research that seeks to impute subjectivity to a closed interior. It insists on the way in which "subjectivity disappears in the recoiling of the origin," leaving us before "the visible void of the origin" (1994: 284). It is in the very suspension of origins that we find words, or that words come to us.

This is then to think childhood and belonging in the terms of the space and time suggested by the phrase "this is not the worst thing I remember." What or where is the worst thing? Does it exist? Is it to come? Images of childhood, from childhood, pull us back to a space that cannot be revisited; they throw us into a present becoming, profoundly disturbing any chronological ordering of life and being. And as I will argue, one of the lines that can be used to scramble this order is that of nostalgia. Nostalgia not as a guarantee of memory but precisely as an errant logic that always goes astray. Nostalgia performed in that empty dimension of childhood freed of its moorings in time. Nostalgia as the impossibility of placing true origins; nostalgia for an irretrievable childhood. A perfidious use that theoretically and affectively constructs a space of experimentation and upsets the space and time of childhood, the naturalness of heterosexual and generational ordering. In this way, childhood may take on its full, visible emptiness—a void that compels other uses of childhood than ones which stake its meaning as originary.

Strange Statistics

But cut to the present, return to the surface in order to reconnoiter the displacements of childhood. As I write, here in Quebec, queer childhood is very much in the air. Far from being free-floating, it is already articulated in tragic and moral tones, evoked in relation to gay and lesbian civil rights, yoked to the suicide toll of young lesbians and gays. This climate is, in part, generated by the increasing visibility of issues concerning lesbian and gay rights. An immediate example can be found in the reaction to a report of the Québec Human Rights Commission on discrimination against gays and lesbians (*De l'illégalité a l'équalité*, May 13, 1994). Hailed as a first in North America, the Commission's report did a fairly commendable job of advocating that the laws of the land measure up to our Charter of Human Rights. (The Quebec Charter was the first in Canada to include sexual orientation.)[1] However, the presentation of the publication was prefaced by the statistic that 40 percent of Canadian adolescent suicides are thought to be committed by gay and lesbian teenagers—a grim figure left hanging during the press conference as neither the Commissioners nor the journalists addressed the issue. Rather, the journalists asked about marriage and adoption, their agenda having been set by a bill the Ontario New Democrats (NDP) were trying to get passed in the Ontario Provincial Assembly. This bill would have given gay and lesbian couples the same rights as heterosexuals, radically altering approximately 50 laws. In turn, it has been the object of some controversy on all sides—including among gay and lesbian groups in Ontario who are fed up with governmental back-pedaling. (What was in the NDP election platform became the object of a free vote.) Members of all parties seized upon the issues of adoption and marital status in order to escalate the homophobic policing of "the family." In a counterattack promoting the bill, Attorney General Marian Boyd used a national literary treasure, *Anne of Green Gables*,[2] as an example of a happy nontraditional family. When that didn't work, she promised to remove the two offending clauses concerning adoption and marital rights "if legislators opposed to it hold their noses and let it pass another vote" (*Montreal Gazette*, June 9, 1994: B1). On June 9, 1994, the bill was finally defeated by a vote of 68–59.

While the upshot of the vote in Ontario and the report in Québec is far from decided, what emerges clearly here are battles fought on the supposedly straightforward ground of childhood: a public panic articulated in terms of two genders on the one hand and same-sex relations on the other. The relevant terminology is, in fact, couples of "opposite genders" as opposed to those of the "same sex." This turn of phrase is far from innocent and neatly lines up with the questions concerning children and adoption—questions frequently conflated (as if we all would rush to reproduce) and collapsed. (Adoption may mean many things, from adopting your girlfriend's child in order to have legal custody in the event of her death to couples or single men and women wishing to adopt a child.) This condensation of different issues plays out in other ways as well. For instance, Québec polls regularly show that, on the one hand, the majority are in favor of gay and lesbian partners receiving the social benefits heterosexuals are entitled to and that, on the other, the majority are opposed to gay and lesbian couples being able either to marry or to adopt. Thus, when it comes to the supposed natural formation of childhood, it seems that a hard-core intransigence lurks beneath contemporary tolerance—that children need homespun examples of the distinct nature of two genders placed in opposition to each other.

This very real gender trouble goes beyond the questionable science of public opinion polls. Lodged within the hard science of sexuality, it is exemplified in quantitative studies that link childhood experience and homosexuality. In these studies, the focus is on gender performance in childhood gauged in terms of gay men's memories of how "gendered" they felt growing up. As Sedgwick has pointed out, "The American Psychiatric Association's much-publicized 1973 decision to drop the pathologizing diagnosis of homosexuality from its next Diagnostic and Statistical Manual (DSM-III) [was followed in 1980 with a] new diagnosis, numbered (for insurance reasons) 302.60: 'Gender Identity Disorder of Childhood'" (1993: 155–156). From that point on, there has been an important move within quantitative psychology to study what is called "gender conforming" and to figure childhood experience as an indicator of future homosexuality. As Jay Paul has recently argued, "The focus and interpretation of research findings on cross-gender behavior in childhood as a sign of broader 'prehomosexual' configuration...have uncritically incorporated our culture's longstanding folk belief in homosexuality as a form of flawed maleness or femaleness" (1993: 42).

I want to turn briefly to the findings of some of the studies that followed the supposed depathologization of homosexuality. While this change of focus demands a thorough analysis of the conceptualization of the relations among gender, sex, and sexuality and a critique of the ways in which psychology has colluded in the configuration of such folk beliefs, what draws me here is quite discrete. I am interested in the general themes that emerge from studies using the "Boyhood Gender Conformity Scale" (BGCS) developed by S. L. Hockenberry and R. E. Billingham—a scale devised as "a measure on which men rate how often they engaged as a child in 10 gender conforming behaviors and 10 gender nonconforming behaviors" (Phillips et al., 1992: 544).

Given that I find the task of describing quantitative research tedious and that the conclusions are depressingly familiar, I beg forbearance. Briefly then, some of the key factors of "normal conformity" are formulated and placed on the BGC scale of importance as follows: "preferred boys' games," "imagined self as sports figure," "imagined self as dancer or model," "preferred girls' games," and (my favorite) "preferred being around older women." Subsequent studies added other supposedly key factors: "considered sissy," "interest in dolls," "engaged in rough-and-tumble play," and "desire to grow up like father" (1992: 544). Perhaps not surprisingly, researchers found that "classification of sexual orientation as an adult on the basis of memory of childhood experiences was more accurate for the heterosexual men than for the homosexual men" (1992: 552). I would take this to mean that straight men can more easily privilege their "normality" in socially sanctioned terms. In other words, the study framed certain gender behaviors as "normal" and proceeded to correlate this "normal" behavior with another "normal" state: heterosexuality. For their part, the authors conclude with a call for more research, arguing that "developmental sequences and paths are of interest, since engaging in some behaviors may systematically increase or decrease the likelihood that other experiences will occur" (1992: 557).

In other words, we need more studies of how not to grow up gay, "sissy or effeminate." Now while I am not a quantitative social scientist, I am enough of a sociologist to question the ease with which such recommendations are made. The reseachers' confidence is especially remarkable given that the key and, as the researchers put it, "powerful discriminators of heterosexual and homosexual men" were "participation in rough-and-tumble play and the desire to grow up like one's father" (1992: 555). As I read this, some very unscientific questions come to mind—such as what planet do these people live on? In a more credible vein, I wonder where variables such as class and ethnicity might fit in, be they expressed in a variety of class-accented homosocial activities or in the wish to differentiate oneself from one's father in a bid for upward (or downward) mobility.

In another study, we turn from fathers to mothers. The article "Maternally Rated Childhood Gender Nonconformity in Homosexuals and Heterosexuals" (Bailey et al., 1993) documents the findings of a study in which mothers were asked to rate their grownup children's "childhood gender nonconformity" (CGN) and the maternal memories were correlated with those of the children. Basically, what the authors want to know is: "Do maternal ratings make a unique contribution in explaining sexual orientation? Or alternatively, do maternal ratings predict sexual orientation through their relationship with self-ratings?" (1993: 467). While this sounds like another riff on the old line "my mother made me a homosexual" (if I give her enough wool, will she make me one too?), at least some women are included. Lesbians are notoriously absent from most of these studies, and in this one the numbers were uneven: 51 heterosexual females and 19 bisexual and homosexual females (with the two lumped together "for brevity"), as opposed to 58 heterosexual men and 83 bisexual and homosexual men. The researchers found that according to the mothers' memories, male homosexuals were "less Masculine and more Nonathletic," while female homosexuals (to continue the researchers' capitalization) were "more Nonconforming, Masculine, Submissive...more Poorly adjusted, less Healthy, and more Passive" (1993: 464). They conclude that "compared to males, results for (homosexual) females were suggestive of a more general nonconformity than mere gender nonconformity" (1993: 468). This then leads the researchers to call for more studies "to demonstrate convincingly whether homosexual females are disproportionately more gender nonconforming during childhood" (1993: 469). Along the way, the researchers might think about explaining a number of striking contradictions, such as how you can be more submissive, more masculine, and more nonconforming all at the same time.

Childhood Tropes

What emerges from these studies is an image of gays as shunning stereotypes of masculinity (not playing football with Dad) and of lesbians as ornery in the face of a binary gender system. Moreover, it proceeds from a naturalized and homogeneous conception of gender: at the most obvious level, one wonders how it is that masculinity in girls results in "bad health" (and indeed what that term may cover), while in boys it results in hearty, rough play. While the methodological labyrinth that supports such studies must be critiqued (it sometimes seems to be their *raison d'être*), such is not my intent here. For as I stress the urgency of analyzing the studies—from their systems of intelligibility to their conditions of possibility, including their funding and dispersal—I do not hold that interdisciplinarity necessarily plays out in an assortment of specialized knowledges, a fluid and fluent movement from one increasingly rarefied domain to another. Rather, I look to the surface and to how such studies coexist with other discourses.

Thus, I want to consider relations of proximity among apparently disparate discursive projects. What concerns me here is the way in which some of the central themes found in these quantitative studies meet up with similar ones in gay and lesbian writing. On one level, this simply points to the fact that pathologizing discourses have materially affected childhood. On another, there is the more complex issue of the ways in which these themes are taken up in gay and lesbian recollections and stories of childhood. In other words, the "folk beliefs" about gender and sexuality that are quantified in psychological research reappear as key narrative elements through which gay and lesbian identity is recited.

In many ways this phenomenon is quite understandable. After all, as postwar America discovered psychiatry and psychoanalysis, several generations of children were sent off to be cured of their homosexuality. And women, struggling with their own "problem that had no name," found themselves portrayed in popular magazines as potential mothers of homosexual boys, as the source or cause of their homosexuality. While this was mainly a middle-class phenomenon, given its popularization in the media it is not surprising that the pathologizing of childhood should reappear as a major moment in recollections of growing up. Anecdotal evidence of the reach of pop-psycho-medical discourses can be heard across any number of stories. For instance, Nancy Kates begins her autobiographical short story by recalling how it had never occurred to her that she had had a "gay childhood": "It took me close to three decades to come out to myself, but my mother had me pegged as a dyke by the age of five" (1993: 126). From five on, Kates's mother did her best to turn her tomboy daughter into a paragon of femininity. When Kates finally came out, her mother admitted that her efforts were "always on the basis of professional advice." In response to her daughter's question about the cruelty of such methods, her mother replied: "I guess it didn't work, did it?" (132).

If Kates's story tells of the affectivity of such psychosexual babble, the difference between gender nonconformity and unqualified nonconformity is crucial in the quantitative accounts. It is a bizarre distinction: try asking yourself at any moment, am I now not conforming (and to what?), or am I now not conforming to the standards of my gender? Even if we slavishly try to conform, it seems that, like the supposed truth of gender, the proto-dyke will out. For instance, I seem to remember, even as a shy kid too chickenshit (or gender conforming) to be a member of the bad-girls gang, being mortified when a headmaster reprimanded me, along with my best friend, for wearing "tight patched jeans." I remember his exact words: "You're nothing but exhibitionists," a severe reprimand for a gentle tendency to flaunt the rules in order to indulge in our innocent tomboy activities.

Not surprisingly, clothes, gender, sex, and desire are often bundled together in many a lesbian's reminiscence of her childhood. Given the ways that schoolgirls are incessantly under surveillance about their dress, a panic fanned by a fear of adolescent female sexuality, clothes can spark off any number of connections.[3] For instance, in the short story "It Happened on Main Street," Linda Heal remembers "sneak[ing] on pairs of shorts under the dresses I resented so...in this adolescent part of my life, when conformity was queen, I stood out quite a bit" (1993: 10). However, in "Jonnieruth," Becky Birtha's story of growing up black and queer, clothes are less a point of contestation than a means of recognition. The protagonist, Jonnieruth, is eight when she first "spied this lady":

> She ain't nobody's mama—I'm sure. And she ain't wearing Sunday clothes. She got on blue jeans and a man's shirt, with the tail hanging out. She got patches on her blue jeans, and she still got her chin stuck out like she some kinda african royalty. (1993: 18)

From this moment on, Jonnieruth has a mission to seek out other places, women, and ways of dressing. She soon finds

> a lady.... She had on this shiny purple shirt and about a million silver bracelets.... Then I spotted this dude coming over.... Looking real fine. Got on a three-piece suit. One of them little caps sitting on a angle. Look like leather. He coming straight over to this lady I'm watching and then she seen him too and she start to smile, but she don't move till he get right up next to her. And then I'm going to look away, cause I can't stand to watch nobody hugging and kissing on each other, but all of a sudden I see it ain't no dude at all. It's another lady. (21)

These examples tell of something more complex than the clinical term *nonconformity* can grasp about lesbians, dress, and desire remembered in later life. What is striking in Birtha's story is the way in which, in memory, several orders of experience come together. In her account, the recognition of "butch" is simultaneously articulated with the equally important recognition of "african royalty" dressed in jeans. These "shocks of recognition" (to borrow Raymond Williams's term) of gender, sexual desire, and identification then play out in a *reconnaissance* of others. This is *reconnaissance* in its double sense: the local process of knowing, a replaying of knowledge; and being recognizant, grateful for the affirmation of what one may have vaguely felt before (desire for a butch, for a femme, for the sight of butch/femme couples). And in this instance, the sighting leads to a reconnoitering: surveying one's childhood locale for other instances of this desire. Fueled by stance, dress, and movement, allowed by the singularity of material conditions, these moments of recognition result in memories that cannot be stratified. No one moment can be privileged as the original cause of desire.

If, as Rosi Braidotti argues, "the affirmation of my subjectivity need not give a propositional content to my sense of identity" (1989: 100), we need to heed the exigencies of why, where, and how one remembers the moments of affirmation that play out as childhood. If desire is remembered, it is also deeply imbricated in the structuring principles of race, class, gender, and place. Given that "learning" or enforcing gender conformity forms an often painful structuration of girlhood, the complexity of gender as event in girls' lives renders the turn of memory more perplexing— and apparently less available to the typing of quantitative research.

In contrast, the scientific categorization of gay boys as "Nonathletic and as less Masculine" turns up repeatedly in gay men's own accounts of their childhoods. In John Preston's anthology *Hometowns: Gay Men Write About Where They Belong* (1992), story after story tells of being too intelligent, of not being a boy's boy, of not liking athletics: "There must have been many ways I was different from the other kids early on. I'm vaguely aware of being too smart, of not being physical enough, of hating sports" (Preston, 1992: 6); "My parents worried that I lacked the masculine qualities.... My peers saw in me a nerdy bookworm who was undoubtedly queer" (Monteagudo, 1992: 14); "I was certain that my family, already puzzled by my silent devotion to books, would reject me entirely if it became known exactly what thoughts occupied my silence" (Nava, 1992: 28).

No doubt the traits of being bad at sports, of being bookish, etc., are important in understanding the trials of growing up gay. But as a way of structuring gay memorial writing, their very commonality makes them problematic. How are we to theorize the singularity of queer uses of child-hood when the memories are cut of the same cloth as the typologies of quantitative social science? At another level, the ease with which one can read queer childhood stories along very general axes is problematic as well. As Margaret Reynolds states in regard to this genre, it "creates its own narrative, but it is a narrative that always covers the same ground, and it is a narrative which becomes an exchange of calling cards within a gay community" (1993: xxvi). "There are masses of them," she adds, and "they are mainly not very good." This, in turn, raises several questions. For one, does the "massiveness" of such tales (a point in their sociological favor) detract from their literary and aesthetic quality? However, I want to ask not so much *why* it is that childhood returns again and again in gay and lesbian writing but *how* that return can be effected differently.

Points of No Return

Going back to childhood is always accompanied by the sheer impossibility of the act. As the adage has it, you can't go home again—or is it that you shouldn't try? Of course, in a compulsive move reminiscent of Freud's "fort-da" scenario, individuals do try to control the uncontrollable object, to retrieve the irretrievable subject of their memories. For example, in Steven Saylor's account of his hometown, place and childhood beckon: "The nostalgia I feel for the place is not just the nostalgia any man feels for the place he came of age; my life there really was rich and sweet and in my daydreams it could be so again" (1993: 122). In contrast, in *Oranges Are Not the Only Fruit*, Jeannette Winterson's autobiographical novel, the return is painfully deployed. The narrator goes back and, sitting in the local tea room, thinks, "There's still a chance that I'm not here at all" (1991: 263). For Winterson, going back entails moving across, a movement fueled by "all the choices I did and didn't make, [which] for a moment brush against each other" (263). If in Saylor's account the past is rosy enough to *want* to go back, in Winterson's novel the past is ambivalent, marked by uneasy coexistence. "'Don't you ever think of going back?' Silly question. There are threads that help you find your way back, and there are threads that intend to pull you back"(247). Even as one wants to return, it is clearly unwise if not fatal: "When Lot's wife looked over her shoulder, she turned into a pillar of salt.... People do go back, but they don't survive.... There is much pain here" (247).

Going back different, going back to people indifferent to your difference, the past indifferent to your present, your presence superfluous to the past, being haunted by places past...there is much pain here. But however painful the actual return may be, the tone in which it is retold introduces epistemological considerations. If Saylor's account brings present and past together in a happy reunion, it also evokes what Foucault calls the "form of history that reintroduces...a suprahistorical perspective...a history that always encourages subjective recognitions and attributes a form of reconciliation to all the displacements of the past" (1977: 152). In this manner, Saylor's nostalgia plays out in the desire for complete reconciliation of past and present; indeed, it is "a history whose perspective on all that precedes it implies the end of time, a completed development" (Foucault, 1977: 152). Being able to control the past means being in control of the present self: the past self mastered through memory grounds the proof of truth in the present. Winterson's account, however, provides a model that privileges the messiness of past, present, and memory. The line of memory here is constantly upset and dislocated by "all the choices I did and didn't make." Brushing against each other, the lines of remembering in Winterson's account jostle "the iron hand of necessity shaking the dice-box of chance" (to recall Nietzsche's evocative phrase). Indeed, *Oranges Are Not the Only Fruit* plays out some very Nietzschean tactics as Winterson remembers her childhood as a profusion of entangled events. Here memory or nostalgia becomes genealogy: a descent which "permits the dissociation of the self, its recognition and displacement as empty synthesis, in liberating a profusion of lost events" (Foucault, 1977: 147). And as Foucault reminds us, "descent attaches itself to the body" (1977: 147). Inscribed in diet, temperament, and soil, it is visible on the bodies of children. Or, in Winterson's tale of memory, descent is written into the construction of relations between her body, her mother's body, and that of her object of desire—all mediated by the orange, an orange genealogically placed next to the apple. The body here is not discovered as the truth of the present; it is in no way a guarantor of things to come. Rather, as Jeannette, the protagonist, puts it, "Some people create themselves afresh outside of their own body.... I have

not gone forward or back in time, but across time, to something I might
have been, playing itself out" (262–263). As a genealogist of her childhood,
Winterson sees there not origin but numberless beginnings, carried, held,
and suspended by lesbian desire.

In his reading of Nietzsche, Foucault argues that *Herkunft*, even
though it is usually translated as "origin," comes close to being the true
objective of genealogy: "*Herkunft* is the equivalent of stock or *descent*; it is the
ancient affiliation to a group, sustained by bonds of blood, tradition or
social class" (1977: 145). Rather than providing a basis for the identification
of generic features, *Herkunft* services genealogy by turning us to the very
unraveling of origin. Again, the notion of beginnings is put to the test of
genealogical analysis and appears not as "the inviolable identity" of origin
but the dissension, the dispersal, the disparity of any and all beginnings.
Rather than re-placing us in direct connection with a comforting, familiar past, genealogy or "the true historical sense confirms our existence
among countless lost events, without a landmark or a point of reference"
(1977: 159). Instead of pristine referents, what we have is the visible and
chaotic void beneath us.

In different registers, Foucault's argument for genealogy and
Winterson's evocation of childhood both return us to the movement of
memory and history as that line which profoundly rearranges any attempt
at ordering origins, at creating order from the point of beginning. We are
faced once again with the project of scrambling modes of putting into play
any reference, any returning, any repealing of the past that comforts the
security of an individualized present. And as Foucault argues, it is in the fictive mode that we most clearly see the necessary distancing, the upheaval
in relations of proximity, that any account of the past produces (and this in
spite of, or to spite the author's intentions). With regard to memory and
writing, Foucault uses the image of "the jutting out of the past, being no
longer the ground upon which we find ourselves—it takes on the stature
of a vertical superposition where the most bygone is paradoxically the closest to the apex, a line of summit, a line of flight, the grounds of reversal"
(1994: 276). Here the past is rendered as a piece of high ground, the underpinnings of which have been washed away. Or again, it is the image of a spatial rearrangement by which the past is bent into strange shapes so that
what should be furthest away is in fact the closest. Put in another way, these

images remind me of the experience of looking through binoculars, a practice I have never mastered: the distant brought disconcertingly forward, I lose all sense of perspective, a faraway landmark (or *point de repère*) suddenly is beside me, a deeply disturbing experience in rearranged proximities.

The point of these images is to indicate that far from being reassuring, the retrieval of the past into the present is profoundly dislocating, disorienting. Bringing forth beginnings results in the loss of bearings. As in Winterson's recollections of childhood, the line of fiction which retrieves her girlhood home produces the pain of the return. In this sense Winterson's tale is precisely nostalgic. Etymologically, the pain of return is, of course, both the condition and the proper definition of nostalgia. Johannes Hofer, a Swiss military doctor who discovered the malady in 1688, combined the Greek terms *nostos* and *algia* to signify "a painful yearning to return home" (cited in Davis, 1979: 1). His list of symptoms included despondency, anorexia, melancholia, lability of emotion, and bouts of weeping (the very symptoms I exhibited the few times I tried to return to a childhood home). In the case of the Swiss soldiers upon whom Hofer based his diagnosis of nostalgia, it was their wish to return home to the Alps and valleys of their youth that precipitated this distressing condition and not the actual return.

But again, you can never go home. Or rather, once returned, you realize the cliché that home is never what it was. I think of those Swiss soldiers returned from the war, cured of their nostalgic pain only to wander their little villages wondering, "Is this all there is?" (Show me the way to the next whisky bar.) As Vladimir Jankélévitch puts it, "Nostalgia oscillates between two regrets: the regret, from afar, of a lost fatherland; the regret, upon return, of missed adventures" (1974: 366). While commonsense understandings of nostalgia tend to emphasize the backward, and even reactionary, nature of nostalgia, Jankélévitch refuses to give nostalgia a fixed political signification. In fact, what is compelling about nostalgia as a form is that it is at once a structure of feeling, a rhetorical strategy, and a historical example of the pathologization of the affections. As Jean Starobinski argues, the medicalization of nostalgia coincides with the general move toward the systematic classification of human affections on the model of botany. Thus, before 1688, amorous melancholia had already been inventoried: "The symptoms and somatic lesions provoked by the privation of the loved object had been described in detail. But this same tradition had never envisioned the troubles resulting from the distancing of a familiar milieu" (1966: 95). However, the condition of *desiderium patriae* came to be considered along with *amorous desiderium* as prime causes of "the mortal effects of chagrin." And it should be remembered that the mortality rate of such affective disturbances was not to be taken lightly. As Starobinski puts it, "Curious XVIIIth century, when the English, in order to cure their *spleen*, fled their native clime and departed on their *grand* tour in search of the serene air of the South—while others thought that they exposed themselves to the risk of death by the simple distancing of familiar landscapes" (1966: 97).

By the end of the eighteenth century this sense of nostalgia as a somatic condition caused directly by the loss of one's place of birth fades into the understanding Kant articulated in his *Anthropologie in pragmatischer Hinsichtabgefasst* (1798), that "what the nostalgic desires is not the *place* of his youth, but youth itself, his childhood. His desire is not directed at a *thing* that could be recovered but towards a time that is irretrievable" (cited in Starobinski, 1966: 106). As Starobinski argues, with the emergence of modern medicine and the study of pathology in the nineteenth century, nostalgia ceases to be understood as a physical condition that could be treated with a local remedy: for Hofer, the remedy had entailed either sending the soldier home or, failing that possibility, the administration of youthful libations—young wine or beer. By the nineteenth century, "the desire to return loses its literal sense" and becomes interiorized: "It is in his personal past that the nostalgic seeks to accomplish a movement of return" (1966: 114). From designating a physical condition, then a psychological one, Starobinski argues that "today, as the imperative to social adaptation grows, nostalgia no longer designates a lost fatherland, but rather goes back to the stages when desire...wasn't condemned to postpone its realization" (1966: 115).

These ideas lead me to argue that in nostalgia we may find a mood that is appropriate to childhood memorial writing. If the reference to childhood is one of nostalgia's immediate meanings, more importantly, it seems to already contain within its history a tension that renders it apt for the expression of queer childhood memories. For nostalgia begins its conceptual career as a discrete objective state, is pathologized, and then falls under the scrutiny of psychology and psychoanalysis to be interiorized as a form of neurosis. But as it passes out of favor within psychology, having done its time within the prism of origins, nostalgia is now free to wander. And according to Jankélévitch, among others, this is precisely what the nostalgic mode does today. As it moves between present and past, nostalgia is no longer tied to an origin or a cause. Rather, like desire, it produces its object. It scrambles any sense of a fixed beginning: "The cause is contradictorily the effect of its own effect, and the effect the cause of its own cause; the *because* refers thus to the *why* and responds to the question with a question" (1974: 356).

While I am not suggesting that nostalgia is the only mode of writing queer childhood, in linking nostalgia, genealogy, and the writing of memory I do propose that we seek to queer the past in the present. Of course this is the project of gay and lesbian historians who have admirably reworked our past histories and conditions of possibility. But it seems that, when the personal past becomes the subject of writing, the past tends to become individualized, grounds for the present truth of selves. If, however, we turn our attention to childhood as event, as a heterogeneous ensemble of discourses and relations, tracing a straight line between a present self as lesbian or gay and any childhood experience becomes somewhat tricky. As a line of descent, the project of recollecting also becomes more pressing as it dissolves, in its own way, the pretense of truth in sexuality.

This Is Not the Worst Thing I Remember

From this teleological scrambling we can start thinking about ways of using and recounting childhood that do not place it as a beginning. This is to move childhood outside a regime of origins, to displace both the question of psychology ("Why is she a lesbian?") and the question that recurs in gay and lesbian narratives of childhood: "Why am I a lesbian?" The point is not to negate the importance of childhood; it is to deny childhood its founding status. It is to rewind our stories but not to recount them as links in a chronological chain that ties the present to a fixed past. It is to tell them with the fervor of the possible, not the implacability of truth-telling. However, it should be clear that in advocating nostalgia as a possible voice for such narrating, I am not proposing that we jettison the reality of childhood, a real that comes to us in images. Rather, I want to seize on those images, images sometimes drenched in the immediacy of past and present pain. It is from this real that we seek to construct the possible, a real that cannot be known solely through statistics and quantitative studies. The reality we must deal with is that of the surface of the social, and we must continue to confront such studies with other representations of gay and lesbian life: images of bodies and desires, history and histories that are central to reformulating the social. For "the possible is only the real with the addition of an act of mind that throws its image back into the past once it has been enacted" (Deleuze, 1989: 17).

Jankélévitch's articulation of nostaligia is based upon a bifurcated movement, upon a sense of a gaze thrown backward and forward, "a germination in the present and a flowering in the past" (1974: 375). While not explicit in *L'irréversible et la nostalgie*, this doubled movement is inspired by Bergson's argument on memory and duration. Indeed, Jankélévitch argues elsewhere that duration informs Bergson's method: "This 'method' would be the line itself of movement that conducts thought into the thickness of things" (1989: 5). In other words, nostalgia becomes a variant of a method that has as its purpose the turning around of things, of rendering the real as the inside-out of past and present. Nostalgia then must be turned around, turned away from its tendency "to practice *a posteriori* a small justifying reconstruction" (1989: 22). For it should be clear that if nostalgia has no inherent meaning or direction, it does have a historical tendency "to represent, in the future anterior, the way in which things should have happened so that they conform to its own schema of immobility" (1989: 21). Against this veering toward an ontology of origins, we need to queer the nostalgic line. For example, in some childhood memorial writing, nostalgia serves merely to replay things as we would want them to be, to rehearse them so that they fall in line with the present. This is the case when, for instance, the question "Why am I gay?" is answered by the response "I was too smart; I was bad at sports." This line of justification is also the narrative that motivates those quantitative studies that calibrate and pathologize memories of "gender nonconformity" in childhood.

In this type of logic there is only one line of movement, one that goes from the present to the past in order to justify the present. To say the least, this is not a very productive line; it does not yield anything new in the present. It merely reproduces the present as an effect of the past, of past causes.

Elspeth Probyn

While this line undoubtedly exists, it must be joined with another line of movement if it is to be productive. It is here that Bergson talks of "two memories—or two indissolubly linked aspects of memory—recollection-memory and contraction-memory" (Deleuze, 1989: 52). For Bergson, "the 'present' that endures divides at each 'instant' into two directions, one oriented and dilated toward the past, the other contracted, contracting toward the future" (Deleuze, 1989: 52). Thus, of the two lines at work in memory, one veers toward the past (recollection-memory) and the other (contraction-memory) is the contracting of "millions of vibrations or elementary shocks into a felt quality; it is the 'tensing' of things into a line of becoming" (1989: 87).

　　While this may sound esoteric, it is, in fact, a mundane activity. Take for instance this example by Bergson: "Sitting on the bank of a river, the flowing of the water, the gliding of a boat or the flight of a bird, the uninterrupted murmur of our deep life, are for us three different things or a single one, at will" (in Deleuze, 1989: 80). Here the line of recollection which bends toward the past (the memory and the actuality of sitting on a bank, the very pastness of a present flowing river and the murmur of life) is redirected and meets up with the contraction of "the millions of vibrations" of these things. Matter is tensed into a felt quality, contracted into a line of memory that may or may not produce these separate fluxes as one. At each point, then, these separate elements (for they must be recognized as such) can veer into the past and organize a present becoming, justifying its order. But, as Deleuze argues, this would be to partake in the past, a past that has "ceased to act or be useful.... It is identical to being itself" (1989: 55). In other words, the past in this sense is that which lifelessly mirrors the present, explains it to itself, or is served up in narratives that encourage a common tale of suffering. The trick is to turn this line, to redirect it alongside the line of contraction so that contraction and recollection exist simultaneously, producing "pure becoming, always outside of itself" (Deleuze, 1989: 55). The point is that we all grow up and in one way or another seek to become other than what we were, what we are.

Suspended Childhood

This explanation of an everyday activity might not be obvious. It is, in any case, already an amalgam of Bergson, Deleuze's explanation of Bergson, and my own attempt to use them in order to think about the movement of nostalgia. That said, I turn to an example that may be clearer than that of Bergson's afternoon on a riverbank. But before I do so, I retain the exigency of conceptualizing the bifurcated movement of remembering childhood; fictions arranged and displayed, they are already conducted in both the past and the present. They move, or can be made to move, us into other modalities of becoming.

If Peck's novel is organized by the phrase "this is not the worst thing I remember," thus placing the reader in suspense, awaiting but never receiving knowledge of what the worst thing is, Michel Tremblay's play *La maison suspendue* (*The Suspended House*) (1990) literalizes the metaphor. One of Québec's best-known authors, Tremblay has always been an out queer, and his work consistently centers on gay characters. Hailed as a sort of Québécois working-class hero for writing the first play in "*joual*" (the street French of Québec), his oeuvre brings together realist accounts of working-class Québécois, drag queens as tragic heros, and a mysticism that always threatens to become maudlin yet never quite does. In his novels and plays he has created and reproduced Québec's queerest extended family, a family that rivals the Addamses. The *Chroniques du plateau*, the cycle of novels that takes place in the East End of the Plateau in Montréal, includes characters like Édouard, a transsexual shoe salesman; Marcel, a mystic kid who plays with his invisible cat, Duplessis (named after the authoritarian premier who ruled over Québec's dark ages before the Quiet Revolution of the 1960s); and incestuous siblings and their offspring.

In *La maison suspendue* Tremblay brings together three generations and three time periods: the characters of Josaphat and Victoire, who are lovers and siblings, and Gabriel, their child, are stituated in 1910; those of *la grosse femme*, Albertine, Édouard, and Marcel are in 1950; and finally, Jean-Marc, Mathieu, and Sebastien are in the present (1990). Jean-Marc, the end of the lineage, has bought his family's old summer house and brought his family to it: his lover, Mathieu, and the lover's son. The play opens with a description of the house, a round wooden house with a porch ("*la galérie*") that circles its exterior. The house gives off "a strange and powerful energy…as if the whole history of the world had unfolded there" (1990: 11). It is the whole of time, the time of his family, that of his new family and the time of his childhood, which causes his lover to ask, "That's why you bought it?

To fall back into childhood?" (11). As he details the comings and goings of generations of his family, Jean-Marc replies, "All this is mine, Mathieu, it's part of my heritage, it's my only heritage.... I bought all those memories so they wouldn't fall into general indifference" (14–15).

The action of the play takes place outside on the gallery one July evening. The major narrative thread is that of Josaphat and Victoire's decision to move to Montréal ("Morial," written just as it is pronounced) so that Victoire can marry Télésphore and thus legitimate Gabriel. Édouard, *la grosse femme*, and Albertine have come for a week, implicitly to help the brother and sister (Édouard and Albertine) get over their differences that are mainly caused by Albertine's shame regarding her brother's queerness. Mathieu has come to help settle in Jean-Marc, who has finally decided to risk giving up his job as a university professor in order to write. The play is pulled along on another level with Josaphat's version of the story of "*la chasse galérie.*" This Québécois fable[4] tells the tale of a bunch of woodsmen who take off for Montréal in search of fun on a Saturday night, their mode of transport being a canoe which is hitched to the moon and that carries them across the night sky. In Josaphat's telling, he makes the moon rise by dint of his fiddle playing and then suspends the house with a cord tied to the moon. While exceedingly simple, the structure of *La maison suspendue* is stunning for the way in which the three generations and three time periods play alongside each other. Characters start a sentence or a thought only to have it finished by another voice from another generation and then to have it extended by yet another. For instance, at one point Mathieu talks of building a new well, catching himself as he does: "My God, I said that as if we're going to spend the rest of our days here." This is followed by *la grosse femme*'s question about what to do with the milk, then by Édouard saying he'll take it down to the creek, which awakens Albertine to the voice of her mother heard from another time. From a moment of connection with her mother, Albertine then turns on Édouard's own recollection of their mother, bitchily remarking, "Ouan.... Just as long as you don't wear her dresses as well." Édouard softly says, "Tiens, that's the first time you allude to that." The stage directions make explicit this intermingling of time and generation: "In turn, he passes between Gabriel and Josaphat, goes around Jean-Marc and Mathieu, and disappears in the creek" (35). In this way, threads weave in and out and alongside each other, the movement being precisely that which Winterson also emphasizes: a commingling of choices made, unmade, and not made, choices virtual and actual that brush against each other. "History is a hammock for swinging and a game for playing. A cat's cradle" (Winterson, 1991: 267). And sure enough, Tremblay's play takes up the metaphor of the suspended house, rendered as the history of three generations of family; a swinging hammock; a cat's cradle of memories, desires, childhood, and grownup queer children.

Tremblay's play exemplifies and puts into motion a use of nostalgia that twists and turns inside-out and outside-in generations of memories. It renders history as a narrative line that, like a Möbius strip, refuses depth. It draws everything to the surface, it spreads the past across the present, it makes the present as flexible as a well-sprung dance floor. The image of the house suspended from the sky, attached by a line of the fiddle, is more than metaphor. It enters into the very structure of feeling that the play enables: a queer desire to render tangible the passage of time, childhood, history, and passion as they brush against each other, creating the *frisson* of surface rubbing surface, the tension of tectonic plates moving. It is descent tied to the body, bodies that desire each other with no thought of trying to fix the origin of desire or body. In Tremblay's world there is no room for the question "Why am I gay?" no possible place from which it could be asked, no thread from the past that would lead to its enunciation. Akin to Bergson's argument, Tremblay tenses matter into memory in such a way that vibrations contract, forcing out any chronological or teleological explanation. The past is not there to explain the present; it is there to encourage forms of becoming. At the end of the play, the only character left is Marcel. Caressing Duplessis, he says to his very real if invisible cat, "We're fine, here.... We're fine, here.... We're fine. We are going...to be...happy" (119). And in the pauses of the ellipses we hear Josaphat's fiddle as it closes to black.

Recommence

To begin again. For some, at times, a dreadful thought, a Sisyphean enterprise. For others, at other times, a project of hope. For if the primary sense of beginning is the time or place at which anything begins, nothing says that those times and places are fixed, no one orders us to start again from where we began the time before, and no one can say where or when the next beginning will occur, or where it may lead. And it is in this simple thought that we find one of the more compelling reasons to mobilize the queer writing of childhood as a political tactic. Compared to the more evident exigencies of repelling the scientific quantification of queer childhood as pathology and of resisting the sustained attempts by governments to capture childhood as their moral high ground, rethinking childhood as the possibility of beginning may sound very abstract. However, it is in rendering evident the very non-necessity, the unnaturalness of the idea of beginning that we may unravel the sacred place that childhood occupies in fixed notions of morality. For while it should be commonplace within theoretical and/or progressive circles to regard childhood as a construct, an entity brought into being by, among other things, the child labor laws of the nineteenth century, when it comes to the writing of childhood, or to Bill Clinton's proposals to help the middle class "because of the children," more often than not childhood passes smoothly into the sacrosanct. There are, of course, important differences between the Democrats' use of children and gay and lesbian writers' use of their own childhood. However, it must be equally clear that when we write of queer childhood, we write within a complex, established, and stratified discursive field of moral meanings of childhood.

Thus, my suggestion to couple the writing of childhood with a reconceptualization of beginnings seeks to unhinge any moralizing necessity and to raise the exigency of extending childhood as a repeatable point of beginning within queer writings. While beginnings form part of our belongings, like memory, they resist ownership. The point then is to deploy these memories of beginnings, of childhood and to turn them in other directions, to place them on the surface of the real and the possible. Nostalgia for beginnings only makes sense within a project that refuses a chronological ground, that refuses the privilege of a personal past as a guarantee of things to come, that explains the present in relation to the past. For the past *is* and what I want *is not yet*. What I want is a present wherein childhood is freed from its moral strictures, where children and adults are not stifled by the confines of a policed family, where grownups can write childhood, live childhood, in whatever order we wish, where we can happily bring up children if we so desire, where images of childhood slowly brush up against other images, where the past quickens a lust for the present and for the possible. As a modest proposal, I would suggest that we suspend childhood, that we formulate a point of departure for theorizing queer beginnings in the very suspension of childhood. Then may we conceive of our beginnings as suspended from the moon, held swaying in place by the thread of a violin, a childhood melody.

5

Disciplinary
Desires
The Outside of Queer Feminist Cultural Studies

Dog Days...

Summer in Montréal, hot and very humid. And as with every year, it seems that the heated pavement brings forth a new Montréal subject, a different social and civic subject wrought of the peculiarities of climate and sensibility. Indeed, it is a local cliché that for a brief moment of time Montrealers and Montréalais alike put off their penchant for politics large and small, cast off with the salt-stained boots and tired coats of winter. The exact timing of the emergence of this fleeting structure of feeling that we call summer can be roughly calculated as somewhere after the Québécois national holiday of St. Jean Baptiste (June 24). Certainly, by July 1, the Canadian national holiday, but more immediately the day that most apartment leases expire, people have started to kick back; sitting on balconies drinking beer, Montréal for the most part celebrates Canada Day by either helping friends move, being helped by friends to move, or watching others move. Of course, politics continues, but it is diverted from its usual route. So yes, *la St. Jean* brings out parades of blue and white "Québec aux Québécois," and in a much less spectacular and numerous way Canada Day has its red "Made in Canada" tee-shirts on display, but these national manifestations are smoothed by many a Labatt Bleue and carried out in the relative ignorance of the one and the other. Even the politicians are savvy enough to know that one doesn't disturb *le peuple* during the summer.

So instead of political platforms we have bandstands; festivals compete and overlap into a weave of carnival, a moving warp of bodies against bodies: the International Festival of Fireworks, the Festival International de Jazz de Montréal, Divers/Cité, the Festival Juste Pour Rire/Just for Laughs, *le festival du homard, le festival de la bière en fût,* le Tour de l'île, Portuguese and Italian saints' days, the Construction Workers' holiday, *les fêtes du trottoir*—all produce the streets as chaotic bursting capillaries of people celebrating something or other, or merely living fully in the forgetfulness that winter ever existed. As an editorial in the local paper puts it, Montréal is a "high-strung city," and a festival "helps a city to put aside its tensions and troubles. Suddenly language doesn't matter. Politics are forgotten. Ethnicity is celebrated, not scorned" (*The Gazette*, July 11, 1994: B-2). So it is that under banners that instruct "Montréal sourit aux touristes," fair-weather subjects proliferate. Both the inhabitants of Montréal and the outside tourists are touched by these municipal dictates to smile and are brought together in a well-planned network of free outdoor shows and inside commercial venues. If summer exuberance is common in places where winter is long and hard, Montréal may be uncommon for the ways in which its citizens are placed within a government-funded web of fun, the exhortations resembling schoolteacherly commands to get out there and play in the rearranged city streets.

And speaking of play, as with every summer, I am literally stuck to my chair, swearing that next summer I won't be tied to my computer— summers of pages, pages of summer. This time, I tell myself, it will be different; I will govern myself differently, produce another social skin. I take Marx to heart, the one who promised that we could do the revolution in the morning and go fishing in the afternoon. My version entails writing in the morning and afternoon, then in the evening participating in the various committees and subcommittees of our local gay and lesbian organization, La Table de Concertation des Lesbiennes et des Gais du Grand Montréal. After which, in the logic that you sweat standing still so you may as well really sweat on the dance floor, it's off to the bars, propelled on my bike in a rush of air and expectation down the hill to the Gay Village.

...and Cat Fights

This goes on for a while, and then, just as we all seem to have concocted a new manner of being, the weather changes, turns really heavy, and electrical storms short-circuit. Catatonia melds people together in an unruly way, alternating between frenzy and lethargy. Tranced-out, supposedly inner thoughts break out on the skin in prickly intellectual rashes. Inevitably the compartments of writing, political organizing, and socializing break down, and comportments get increasingly cataleptic. At a party, I rub shoulders with presumed comrades-in-arms, and talk turns around issues of a renewed gay and lesbian civic presence, Divers/Cité (our queer pride festival), the fact that we have a South American butch as the new president of the main gay and lesbian organization, projects and political challenges. Slightly bored and certainly damp, I seem to recall saying something mundane about the necessity of having more diversity in our ranks, of working in concert with the other communities, other universities, etc. Abruptly, it seems, one of my companions is in full *parti pris* grandstanding. The tenor of his rage is language, the vehicle queer theory and political correctness, which he takes to be typically anglophone, propagated by what he terms hypocritical "white Rhodesians" (the rallying separatist cry of the 1970s against *les anglais*) who talk of difference yet refuse to speak French. In response, I rally to the defense of queer theory, attacking his conception of "*les études gaies et lesbiennes*" as impossibly parochial. Even on a summer night politics hasn't disappeared, it has merely taken another route by which to emerge.

All in all, not a pretty performance, but in the local and linguistic terms of gay, lesbian, and queer politics, not an unusual one. In turn, our little exchange fits all too easily within a larger theoretical climate. For in the world of sexual politics, it seems that "queer" has become the latest lightning rod, attracting straights, gays, lesbians, and bisexuals alike in a common clucking over the loss of politics that the very term is taken as inaugurating. This argument runs in drearily familiar ways and recalls similar types of arguments mounted against feminism and cultural studies, most clearly carried through the divisions for and against postmodernism and poststructuralism. In fact, the terms of the attack don't seem to have changed as queer theory is dissed for its lack of politics, its occulting of the social, its insistence on the local, and its privileging of discourse. *Déjà-vu*, the mode of argumentation seems ready to roll along the same type of defensive, negative positioning as the battle lines are set up between gay and lesbian and queer, defenders and attackers ranged in preset formations. Lest my tone suggest *ennui*, I do think that the stakes underlying this current scenario are incredibly important, and in particular, I want to work against the potential and further dissipation of much-needed critical, intellectual energies within our academic institutions. Epochal grandiloquence aside, the present conjecture demands that we revitalize and reformulate the point and direction of academic political interventions within the actual social terrain of sexuality.

In entering into the fray, I want to be clear about the point of my own engagement. For I am less interested in carrying on frontal attacks on either the proponents of queer theory or those in opposition to it than I am in articulating a slightly different project. Quite simply, queer theory *in general* no longer overly interests me. And even if I take cultural studies as my point of departure, it is a slippery one in that cultural studies *in general* is notoriously difficult to pin down. What I want to do here is to conjugate a number of theoretical lines that interweave feminism; cultural studies; gay, lesbian, and queer studies in order to conceive of sexuality, sexual practices, and sexual belongings as constituting a certain threshold today: to place sexuality as the point at which various systems that regulate the social (from academic disciplines to governmental policy initiatives) are openly displayed. In tentatively thinking out loud about a possible program, I do not seek to propose a normative path for the future of queer studies but rather, to put forth that hazardous, if more limited, question: What program can queer cultural feminist studies articulate faced with the plethora of questions, statements, and objections about sexuality? I am here hijacking the concept of program, but only very slightly. For if within a problematic of governmentality, programs "are not simply formulations of wishes or intentions," they do "lay claim to a certain knowledge of the sphere or problem to be addressed" (Rose and Miller, 1992: 182). Against a vertical model of ascending depths, it strikes me that we are currently imbricated in a surface model: knowledges, objects, ideas no longer drip or trickle down (if they ever did); rather, they translate, move and creep across, are creased and folded into other shapes.

As a programmatic argument that seeks to figure actual and virtual directions, this is to bring together social tendencies, to trace the ways in which they may play out in shifting the grounds of belonging. Rather than sedimenting one point of departure from which one would then look upon what is happening, I want to move laterally—to be caught up in the lateral movement of disciplines, to construct an object of study both included within the larger framework of cultural studies yet having a certain autonomy in the construction of its objects and its mode of intervention. This program is then not a blueprint but one possible way of negotiating the theoretical present. As a strategic writing practice it attempts to embody certain notions and directions and to tug at others to see if they may be led astray. It is committed to the positivity of thought, to the ways that words have in sparking off others.

As I have argued throughout this book, the problematic of outside belonging necessitates rendering singular both the object and the mode of inquiry. Amidst the range of the theoretical specificities of feminist, queer, cultural studies, I endeavor to forge one singular example of thinking in the face of certain contingencies. If I have tried to put various theoretical insights to work in the service of figuring the interconnections of sex, desire, and belonging with other objects on the surface, here I turn to thinking about a theoretical network or topology: queer feminist cultural studies, at once a totally idiosyncratic programmatic proposal and a mode of theorizing dependent on larger disciplinary formations as it attempts another way of positioning the stakes involved in its own theorizing. While it may seem a bit backward to conclude with a program, it is also concomi-tant with my argument that larger epistemological questions rise to the surface in the process of singularizing local examples.

I am far from proposing that this program would be unique; on the contrary, I want to emphasize the necessary interdisciplinarity and even intersociality of any contemporary project of cultural critique. And I would be the first to admit that the nomenclature of queer-feminist-cultural studies is unwieldy both aesthetically and epistemologically. For a start, queer and feminist and cultural studies are already embroiled in each other, and in a few years' time it may be simply redundant to have to name each element. However, for the time being, it seems that it is neces-sary to denote the specificities, hoping that the singularity of the project may emerge in its actual engagement. Following Williams's sense of engagement, I refer to the challenge of thinking and working in the inter-twined terms of "project" and "formation." As he argues, "You cannot understand an intellectual or artistic project without understanding its formation.... Project and formation are different ways of materializing—different ways, then, of describing—what is in fact a *common* disposition of energy and direction" (1989: 152). In his article "The Future of Cultural Studies," Williams delineates the point of cultural studies' intervention as merely another form, a different direction, of the line of the social that it studies. Thus, "'project' and 'formation' are addressing not the relations between two separate entities...but processes which take these different material forms in social formations" (1989: 52). In part based on his experi-ence of the Workers Education Association (WEA), a project obviously embedded in its formation, Williams writes that "intellectual questions arose when you drew up intellectual disciplines that form bodies of knowledge in contact with people's life-situations and life-experiences" (1989: 156). In his inimitable way, Williams returns us to the very difficulty of such a project, stating that the project of WEA "was based precisely on a principle which it could not realize" (1989: 156).

It is in this manner, as a wager, that I propose a topology of conjugated lines of analysis that would find its singularity in the particular articulation of sexuality within the production and reproduction of the relations involved in governing the social. What interests me here is the point, or the produced space of articulation, between self-governance and governmentality that I pose as the outside of our studies. This is to position queer feminist cultural studies within and through the optic of governmentality in order to figure the constitution of the terrain in which, as an intellectual project, it would intervene. That terrain can be defined in broad terms as concerning

> the relation between self and self, private interpersonal relations involving some form of control or guidance, relations within social institutions and communities and, finally, relations concerned with the exercise of political sovereignty...the interconnections between these different forms and meanings of government. (Gordon, 1991: 2–3)

This leads me to place sexual belongings as a privileged instance of "'the conduct of conduct': that is to say, a form of activity aiming to shape, guide or affect the conduct of some person or persons.... 'The government of one's self and of others'" (Foucault, cited in Gordon, 1991: 2). Following from these statements, I would then set the sexual government of oneself and others within the broader frame of the interrelations of institutions, forms of governing, the role of academic disciplines, modes of analysis, and the interface of local political actions with those of government policies.

As is abundantly clear, I want the concept of the outside to do several orders of things. One of my immediate preoccupations is to work against a current rarefication of academic endeavors whereby certain objects of study are made to belong exclusively to certain fields, and even to individual researchers. Along with this possessiveness, there seems to be an increasing narrowmindedness which can be observed in the routine denunciations of other work and a certain ignorance of how objects of study get produced. This negates proper interdisciplinary endeavor, a mode of inquiry that would seek the singularity of the objects under study, a program that would encourage the commingling of singularities. If the outside of theoretical work can be seen to be produced in the historical intermingling of objects of study, we need to recognize the ways in which objects of study carry the determinations of their historical conditions of emergence, to see them as artifacts which can be made to reveal how, at various points of time, scientific, popular, and governmental interests are encapsulated and conceptualized. As an initial proposition, this is to figure disciplines and modes of theorizing so that their fundamental exteriority meets up with the objects that they have historically produced. Beyond individual possessiveness, this is to place ourselves as parts or cogs within machinic systems of critical reflection: as Grosz puts it, "The point is, that part of what we do is invested in the very system we want to critique" (1994c: 9). This is a first step in realizing that "the problem is posed to concepts, to thinking, from/as the outside that can only appear to thought as the unthought.... The outside insinuates itself into thought, drawing knowledge outside of itself, outside of what is expected" (Grosz, 1995: 133).

This challenging problematic entails a close attention to the relations of proximity between concepts, institutions, and social practices: "For each historical formation, one has to ask what belongs to each institution existing on a particular stratum, which is to say, what relations of power does it integrate, what relations does it have with other institutions and how do these repartitions change from one stratum to another?" (Deleuze, 1986: 82). To clarify, consider Deleuze's explication of Foucault's analysis of the elaboration of scientific disciplines:

> The human sciences are not separable from the relations of power which render them possible, and which instigate knowledges more or less capable of overcoming an epistemological threshold or of forming ways of knowing: for example, for a "sciencia sexualis," the relation of penitent-confessor, faithful, director; or for psychology, disciplinary relations. This is not to say that the human sciences come from the prison, but that they suppose the diagram of forces upon which the prison itself depends. (1986: 81)

By now this description of the imbrication of ways of knowing, of objects of knowledge, institutions, and relations of power should be evident, yet it bears repeating that the human sciences must be held accountable for their conduct and productions. While not a causality whereby a particular disciple directly produces a social effect (although it has been known to happen), disciplines are always imbricated within and suppose a diagram of forces: a web of "relations of power [which] are the differential relations that determine singularities (affects)" (Deleuze, 1986: 82). It seems to me that moving within such webs, one hears not only the history of a discipline, what is considered to be its constituent interior, its ontology, but also the way in which it mobilizes its interior anteriority as its public *raison d'être*. This point of tension then opens up research to outside questioning. For instance, the discipline of sociology which has historically produced certain forms of sociality is now held accountable for the ways it increasingly inadequately intervenes in the social. As Jacques Donzelot has argued, societal "crisis" is in fact imbricated in the very origins of sociology as discipline and succor. As one line in the gradual integration of different concerns and concepts that became something called sociology, Donzelot notes that at the end of the 1880s, "organized around the idea of solidarity, [it] claims to provide both a theory of society and a technique for solving social problems which harmonize perfectly with each other" (1993: 109).

This harmonizing of theory and technique, discipline and concern, then forms part of the outside of sociology, an outside that is evidently fully social. Like Gianni Vattimo's notion of a "weak horizon," "we discretely displace ourselves" (Vattimo, 1987: 19) on the outside, finding a surface upon which is arranged any number of objects produced as public domains of concern. The public nature of the outside raises the exigency of working with a certain *"justesse"* (exactness, appropriateness), of constantly evaluating the degrees of proximity between concepts, and objects, in order to more adequately hone theoretical interventions. It is work conducted along with the demands for accountability (and *justesse*) from both within the discipline and from without: demands that may take any number of forms—those of students and colleagues, the media, the demands of local political organizations, government directives, funding requirements, and so forth. The outside is then that meeting place of supposedly internal disciplinary questions and the so-called external articulations of social exigencies.

Of course, the production of the discipline as outside is not a stable undertaking but rather proceeds at different times and under the pressure of different contexts. Furthermore, it is far from inevitable that disciplines turn inside out, the outside being precisely a production, the result of theoretical and political work. As an instance of the type of theoretical activity that interests me, the work of Meaghan Morris is exemplary for the way that she consistently draws attention to, and contributes to, the production of a certain outside. Beyond her own biography, which has placed her as an independent scholar, a former newspaper film critic, etc., Morris draws out the necessary interconnections among economic relations, the specific development of Australian nation-ness, the roles of women and sexual politics, cultural production and representation, the deployment of space and place, etc. It is a mode that refuses disciplinary insiderness while imbricating tough epistemological questions with everyday concerns. Consider, for instance, the following exchange in which Morris responds to charges from *within* cultural studies that cultural studies as a discipline must be directed to the supposedly immediate and real questions of cultural policy in Australia. Although much of her work is precisely aimed at intervening in policy debates, she nonetheless refuses a vision of cultural studies as "'analysis of and for policy.'" To this type of exhortation whereby some individual concerns are said to be public while feminist concerns are merely internal, private intellectual affairs, Morris succinctly replies, "For feminists there is always a critical 'outside' to any professional activity— namely, the complex reality of feminism" (1992: 546). In turn, the "outside" is in part constituted through the "unpredictable and even unwelcome 'third term' of *outsider* feminist criticism.... Consequently, feminist theorizing...rarely falls for the kind of binary logic now driving the policy polemic into manichean battle with an imaginary 'critical' Other." In her deft way, Morris turns the tables on insider articulations that place feminist concerns as somehow less social, as more outside real concerns, than policy studies.[1] Rather, it is this type of knowing rhetoric that is more properly internal to disciplines.

Against the inflation of the real and the social as abstract ideals, it is clear that we desperately need some new or renewed chronotopes, optics for reading "as x-rays...the forces at work in the culture system from which they spring" (Bakhtin, cited in Gilroy, 1993: 225 fn). Take the example of Paul Gilroy's recent book, which is explicitly posed against what he calls "rhetorical strategies of 'cultural insiderism'" which seek to fix the outside of identities through and in "an absolute sense of ethnic difference" (1993: 4). Gilroy's chronotope is that of the "black Atlantic" and of the ships that traversed and produced her as such: "the image of the ship—a living, micro-cultural, micro-political system in motion" (1993: 4). Instead of a "relationship of identity to roots and rootedness," Gilroy argues that "the history of the black Atlantic...continually criss-crossed by the movements of black people not only as commodities but engaged in various struggles towards emancipation, autonomy and citizenship—provides a means to examine the problems of nationality, location, identity and historical memory" (1993: 16). Gilroy effects a profound rethinking of the spatial and temporal ordering of black belonging and of the epistemological belongings of black nationalism and African-American studies. He splays the inner workings of historical oppression and renders them visible as exterior forms of sociality created in the movement back and forth on the Atlantic, immediately and symbolically producing external and material forms of black subjectification. While acknowledging the importance of how historical technologies of oppression seek to instill internalized modes of being, Gilroy departs from a dominant psychological depth model of racialized subjectivity, just as he parts from that of radical constructionists. The extraordinary *"justesse"* of Gilroy's work is to be seen in the way in which it brings together the specificity of the historical fact and experience of oppression while refusing to allow that experience to be figured as the stable interior possession of either individuals or fields of study. With the image of the ship on and within the workings of the black Atlantic, Gilroy critically extends the concept of diaspora, ridding it of its connotation of an original point of departure.

Gilroy's argument theorizes the singularity of black Atlantic identity and forms of black subjectification as formed within the historical and material folds of the Atlantic—the moving and unstable terrain of the commerce in bodies, subjectivities, nations, and empires. As I take from its singularity, I am inspired not to generalize to other historical forms of oppression but rather to think in its terms of movement across. To reconsider how the lateral movements of the black Atlantic lap upon the construction of sexuality; to remember that in the ports of Liverpool and elsewhere the sexuality of black men and white working-class women were constructed as coterminous, as the extreme poles within which all other sexualities were to be conceived (Bland and Mort, 1984). As with a fresh fig, Gilroy peels back and lays bare the folds of "movement and mediation" (1993: 19) exteriorized on the surface of history; it is an analytic optic that profoundly skews arguments about identity that proceed through the dichotomization of the local and the global, the discursive and the material.

If Gilroy gives us the black Atlantic as the outside, the surface upon which historical and contemporary productions of black subjectification interconnect with technologies of oppression, within gay and lesbian cultures the outside has been seen as both the site of oppression and as a liberatory space. Indeed, a common trope, its polyvalency is both a help and a hindrance. As Diana Fuss argues, "Interrogating the position of 'outsiderness' is where much recent lesbian and gay theory begins, implicitly if not always directly raising the questions of the complicated processes by which sexual borders are constructed, sexual identities assigned, and sexual politics formulated" (1991: 2). While important, to my mind Fuss's argument has a normative weight that is confusing: "To be out is to finally be outside of exteriority and all the exclusions and deprivations such outsiderness imposes" (1991: 4). Notwithstanding the evident necessity of recognizing the risks imposed by being out or being closeted, Fuss's argument is predicated on a Lacanian-inspired formulation of the lack. The lack becomes that which guarantees the barriers separating the inside and outside: "Any outside is formulated as a consequence of a lack *internal* to the system it supplements" (1991: 3).

This spatial modeling then replays the outside as the mirror of the internal working of the system and, I think, despite Fuss's efforts, does not quite disable the type of rhetoric she wants to avoid: "Does inhabiting the inside always imply cooptation?. . . And does inhabiting the outside always and everywhere guarantee radicality?" (1991: 5). These types of questions will continue to flow from a model whereby the inside becomes the internal, the locus which defines the outside. There is a schism in her argument which acts as the condition of possibility for the distinction between interior states and exterior actions, even as she tries to redefine such opposi-tions. Cognizant of Fuss's intervention, I nonetheless seek to propose another framework and to argue that this spatial arrangement of inside/out be flattened, that we regard the outside as the welding of the interior and exterior.

The Rise of the Queer...

Being out, becoming out, being in: from the perspective of an outsider, the rapidity of the ascendency of queer studies must seem quite astonishing. Accounts of its emergence vary: Eric Savoy dates it, as he says somewhat arbitrarily, from the 1991 Lesbian and Gay Studies Conference at Rutgers University, while in her introduction to *The Lesbian Postmodern*, Robyn Wiegman portrays queer theory as "a term coined, it seems by Teresa de Lauretis" (1994: 17). And as Savoy notes, *queer* quickly took on a "performa-tive role as a defiant adjective" (1994: 129). Indeed, one could say that per-ceptions of overnight success and popularity form part of the outside of queer studies. It matters little if they are indeed exact—a bewildered col-league of mine recently commented that a sociology conference had fea-tured queer issues in every second session, an assertion which turned out to be total fantasy. However, it is germane to remember that at the marathon Cultural Studies Now and in the Future Conference held in 1990, Jan Zita Grover could quite correctly ask about the total absence of papers dealing with issues of gay and lesbian sexuality. While there were two important papers (one by Grover herself, the other by Douglas Crimp) on AIDS, Crimp argued in the discussion following his paper, "The inclu-sion of discussions of AIDS within a cultural studies conference must not be taken as an inclusion of queer sexuality" (1992: 132). A few years later, if the question of what constitutes cultural studies remains open, the visibil-ity of queers in cultural studies is for the moment assured. Along with con-ferences like Console-ing Passions, where, following the cue of Alexander Doty (1993), there are queer Lucys, Lavernes, and Shirleys, there are now queer sessions at relatively staid conferences. By 1993 not only had a small avalanche of queer books been published but they had also been reviewed. And, as Sherri Paris put it, reviewing Judith Roof's *A Lure for Knowledge* (1991) and Fuss's edited *Inside/out* (1991), "What is bold, and might have been radi-cal, about these books is the claim they have in common: that they are lesbian and gay perspectives on theory rather than theoretical works about lesbians and gay men" (Paris, 1993: 984).

...and the Fall of the Social

While Paris's thoughtful comments recall the history of feminist questions about the difference between books on women as opposed to feminist books, I would like to shift the focus of her remarks. For the mode of writing that I propose refuses the possibility of writing "on" and argues for writing within objects, placing oneself on the same surface. As I argued earlier, this entails a commitment to becoming-other in writing: a dissolution between entities that scrambles the distinction between writing "on" and writing "about"—a challenge to become-other than the author in front of the object.

Another problem posed by the distinction that Paris raises is that it returns us to a situation where writers are policed for proof of their right to belong, or what Savoy calls "the obsession with difference" (1994: 143), an obsession that quickly becomes a fixation on the terms of entry and one that is conducted at the expense of figuring the point of intervention. If it isn't clear enough that we hardly need yet more policing, I turn to two recent reviews of queer theory that seek to set out what should be the proper object of study of queer cultural studies. If I am loath to discuss the respective articles by Rosemary Hennessy and Donald Morton because of their relentless negativity, their characterization of certain key terms threatens to further fuel an already dichotomous and divisive situation within cultural theory.

Hennessy's review essay plays Monique Wittig's *The Straight Mind* against the special issue of *differences* on "Queer Theory: Lesbian and Gay Sexualities," edited by de Lauretis. However, if Wittig is apparently more favored than de Lauretis, she in fact gets short shrift. Hennessey's review would have been an ideal opportunity to take up previous questions in order to display them together on a surface, in their full cross-fertilization. For instance, one would thus consider how Wittig's "straight mind" is most fully comprehended in reference to Guillaumin's argument against difference, which is in turn mobilized not to the question of lesbian sex but to the construction of racism (1995). On the same surface, we would find de Lauretis's arguments about the very materiality of experience within the working of the ideology of gender, an argument that turns Althusser on his head while keeping a grounding in the quotidian experience of gender—an argument that predates her work on lesbian representation but is essential to understanding it.

However, Hennessy foregoes a surface genealogy of queer thinking and poses an interconnected body of thought less as a project and more as a pastime: "The terms in which social relations and sexuality in particular, are imagined by queer theorists...[is through] an emphasis on queer identities, on the discursive or symbolic dimensions of the social, and on sexuality as erotic pleasure or play" (1993: 965). In contrast, materialist feminists are said to "maintain that the fragmentation of the subject in the age of information and the function of sexuality in the formation of complex, unstable, and multiple subjectivities cannot be theorized very effectively without coming to terms with the systematic operations of capitalism and patriarchy" (1993: 965).

If this characterization of the two does not make it clear enough that for Hennessy materialist feminists are concerned with real and pressing issues while queer theorists are just playing around, the rest of the article is taken up with the argument that queer theory evacuates the social and collapses it into the cultural: "At stake here is queer theory's implicit conception of the social...the social is consistently conceptualized as only a matter of representation, of discursive and symbolic relations" (1993: 968). In a nutshell, and reminiscent of common critiques of cultural studies in general, Hennessy sums up queer theory as "the 'bad subject' who refuses or negates the dominant culture but in so doing does not necessarily address the larger social arrangements in which culture participates... queer theory presumes that cultural change is commensurate with social change" (1993: 971).

Now it is certainly not my aim to defend all of queer theory against such criticisms, nor even de Lauretis's issue of *differences*; rather, it is the terms of Hennessy's argument that I take issue with, and this on a number of levels. For a start, her unproductive opposing of the social versus the cultural, the local versus the global, the economic versus the symbolic, the real versus the discursive does not constitute a viable alternative to the disciplinary matters she takes to task. If indeed, as she argues, we need to focus on the systematic operations that produce normative sexuality, rendering abject a series of operators will not get us any closer to her goal. In turn, the separation of different spheres and their consequent hierarchization in terms of a supposed political significance does not even come close to a commonsense understanding of how the world works. I am not suggesting that all is cultural or symbolic; what I am arguing is that in order to figure the work of the cultural in the social we need to discretely trace their singular lines of force at any given moment. This is to take up the challenge of rethinking the very terms of the social and cultural: to place sexuality within their interalignments, the diagram of forces that produce at given times the spaces in which change and the nature of the social can be considered and reconceived.

If the terms that Hennessy privileges are unequal to the task of grasping the current interarticulation of social and cultural forces that produce sexuality as a very public and outside domain, Morton's article on the politics of queer theory uses a similar vocabulary as he mobilizes it against the category of experience. From within his own neomarxist perspective, he characterizes *any* project that seeks to work with experience as "ludic," thus writing off the sustained theoretical and conceptual rethinking of the reach of experience within cultural studies, feminism, gay, lesbian, and queer theories. This quite considerable task is done with bravado: "Throughout this essay I have refused to follow the ludic (post)modern mode of acquiring authority for my critique by locating it in the contingencies of (personal) 'experience.'... I have not, in other words, deployed my identity as a gay person as a theoretical axis" (1993: 142).

While Morton is of course free to do with his sexuality what he may, this willful rendering of "experience" and "identity" as equivalent occludes the epistemological and political history of how these terms have been variously put to work. This erasure of the anteriority of theoretical concepts continues elsewhere in his article. For instance, he is quite vicious about the attempt to put sensuality to work in figuring the immediacy of the material and names it as a quality of queer theory to be deplored. However, the sensual has been put in the service of more closely describing the materiality of certain structures of feeling as a strategy within cultural studies, initiated by such unqueer theorists as Williams (notably, in his use of the "shock of recognition" but also in his protracted discussions about the positivity of emotions [1979]) and Richard Hoggart (in his tactile tracing out of the autobiographical and the social [1963]). For Morton this is mere class privilege: "The distinguishing feature of 'queer' Queer Theory is its ludic grounding in the sensory...the latest version of bourgeois ideology in the domain of sexuality" (1993: 139).

Perhaps the most telling specter that Morton deploys against queer theory is the normatively weighted notion of "cooption":

> Queer Theory is rapidly following the path taken by most other marginal groups (feminists, African-Americanists, and so on) and is joining with the dominant form of (post)modern theory and its mode of cultural investigation, which privilege politically unreproductive understandings of such categories as 'desire,' 'discourse,' and the 'material.' (1993: 123)

Clearly, the key terms here come to us via Morton's articulation of postmodernism. And while Morton is not alone in his division of postmodernism into on the one hand resistant and on the other ludic, to my knowledge he is the first to divide cultural studies into two opposing domains: "experiential" versus "classic"/"critical": "Unlike experiential cultural studies, whose mode is 'descriptive' and whose effect is to give the (native) bourgeois student of culture the pleasure of encounter with the exotic 'other,' the mode of critical cultural studies is 'explanatory'...to produce socially transformative cultural understandings" (1993: 125).

The thread that runs through Morton's argument is that most of cultural studies and all of queer studies are taken up with "the local" as opposed to "the social." The local is then taken as blocking "a dialectical historical knowledge of the social totality...[queer theory produces] merely a reformist politics" (1993: 122). But not only is queer cultural theory reformist, it actually "dissolves sociality" (1993: 137). In contrast to the bourgeois ideology that passes in the name of queer ludic, experiential cultural studies, "what is required, instead, as resistance (post)modernism and critical cultural studies insists is subject-citizens 'mobilized' as partisans in the task of radical, system-wide (not merely local) social transformation" (1993: 138).

As is the case with polemics, Morton never actually goes beyond mobilizing his oppositions in order to give us a sustained argument, an exposition, or even an example of his version of cultural analysis. And as

Foucault notes in regard to the genre of the polemic (one which he abhorred for its derouting of the search for truth and its hostility to others), "Polemics defines alliances, recruits partisans...it establishes the other as an enemy, an upholder of opposed interests against which one must fight until the moment this enemy is defeated and either surrenders or disappears" (1984b: 382–383). If it is quite clear that in Morton's argument queer, ludic, experiential cultural studies are posed as the enemy, heralding the return of the bourgeois subject and thus positing Morton himself as the defender of radical, nonreformist thought, the hero of truly oppressed peoples and of the social; it is less than obvious with whom he wishes to form alliances, or where he seeks partisans to his cause.[2]

Strangely enough, in that Morton wishes to place himself as the outsider, his argument in actual fact is very insiderist. Moreover, for an avowed materialist, he mobilizes a conceptual vocabulary ("the structure of the social totality," "class interests," "subject-citizens") as if these concepts immanently pointed to an always-already constituted ground. At the same time that that ground is rendered as self-evident, accusations fly. As Rosalind Brunt characterizes this type of argumentation, "Any attempt to use a politics of identity to render a more rigorous and dynamic concept of class" is automatically met with cries of "'You're abandoning class; you've lost faith in the working people'" (1989: 150). The problem with such recriminations, and Hennessy's and Morton's more sophisticated versions, is that they tend to be presented as evident, as *really* real. But these statements that invoke the social are most often bereft of bodies; critiques are personalized against individual theorists, but the supposed motivation for such critiques is carried out in the name of very nebulous groups. One of the central problems with such a discourse is that it ignores the thrust of the question that Brunt takes from Gramsci—of "how to make a politics that was subjectively relevant" (Brunt, 1989: 153). In turn she argues that we need to "reflect on why and how people become political in the first place or indeed, drop out of politics or shift to different positions" (1989: 152). These very pragmatic questions are often put aside by those who accuse others of forgetting the political, to the extent that one wonders if such critics actually spend much time in the frankly quite humdrum, often incredibly time- and energy-consuming process of "doing" politics (the question of what constitutes "doing politics" is obviously a large one).

But instead of taking for granted why people might want to spend, say, a beautiful summer evening inside around a kitchen table organizing some political manifestation or another, it is time we got real about "politics as a process of social formation and not some given fact of nature" (Brunt, 1989: 152). It's time we got going about "recognising the degree to which political activity and effort involves a continuous process of making and re-making ourselves—and our selves in relation to others" (Brunt, 1989: 151).

Getting Real about the Social

If we need to think in terms of making politics subjectively relevant, it is equally crucial that we also think about making the sexual socially relevant. This entails asking after and locating "the gap now between the actual and potential political subject" (Brunt, 1989: 159). This is importantly different from the gist of the critiques leveled at queer studies and cultural studies, i.e., that these forms of theorizing are exclusively invested in formulating a disembodied subject created in resistance to, or in pleasure with, forms of cultural consumption. In the stead of such claims, rendering politics, the social, and the sexual subject relevant requires that we encourage interconnections, not further compartmentalization. Instead of an "add-on" model whereby sexuality, gender, or race are appended to an empty category called "the political subject," we need to analyze and encourage the productions of social subjects through sexuality, politics, etc. This includes a more generous consideration of how individuals may be "outed" despite themselves—thrust into an outside role because of the ways in which sexuality is represented, ordered, or condoned on the social surface. In this vein, there are a lot of gays and lesbians who are less than pleased with the current situation whereby the combination of media, legal, medical, governmental, private industry, and intellectual attentions are producing them as political in the name of their sexual practices. To say the least, a vocabulary of cooption and individual culpability does nothing to actualize sexuality as a mode of becoming a political subject, nor does it clarify the political stakes at hand.

To give Morton his due, it has to be said that there are some analyses that focus obsessively on certain forms of mass culture, only to make large claims about the production of subjectivity—sexual and otherwise—analyses such as Doty's *Making Things Perfectly Queer* (1993) that seem to run on whim rather than through any solid thought about the relation of cultural production to possible forms of social reproduction. Doty's book has certainly had an impact and is entertaining; however, it is also a blatant example of "cultural insiderism," both theoretical and geopolitical, as Doty takes as evident the assumption that queer readings of American television shows are intrinsically interesting to the world at large. Moreover, as Doty says of his analyses, "these queer readings seem to be expressions of queer perspectives from the inside, rather than descriptions of how 'they' (gays and/or lesbians, usually) respond to, use, or are depicted in mass culture" (1993: 3). Texts are subjected to a "deep" reading rather than being opened up to their outside. It is, to return to the terms of Hall's encoding/decoding argument which is acknowledged as informing Doty's analysis, a series of decodings on Doty's part, but one whereby the complex processes of encoding and the social determinations and limits of decoding are ignored. In fact, these individualized readings are only possible if the moment of decoding is truncated and extracted from the historicity of the very circuit of encoding and decoding. In turn, this type of reading can be conducted only if one discards Hall's protracted discussion of the nature of the ideological work of language and codes and his painstaking route through Marx, Gramsci, and Althusser to arrive at the encoding/decoding model. Thus, any contemplation of decodings—dominant or queer—must first and foremost contend with "the underwiring and underpinning of that *structured ideological field* in which the positions play, and over which, so to speak, they 'contend'" (Hall, 1977: 346). In this vein, studies like Caren Kaplan's analysis of *I Love Lucy* aim precisely at an outside reading of television sitcoms, placing them on a surface that also proffered, among other things, the "Good Neighbor" policy along with depictions of Latin sexuality, thus providing a grounded study of the interproduction of domestic and geopolitical space (Kaplan, 1994). This type of work that figures sexuality as an outside concern can be seen in Lauren Berlant's study of "infantile citizenship" (1995), which draws out the interconnections among *The Simpsons*, queer sexuality, and present and past US government policy and precisely elucidates the conditions of encoding of American television and raises the stakes on the *limits* of social decoding, effects, and affect. Thus, instead of writing off culture, dismissing discourse, and reifying the real, what we need are more analyses like these of the current articulations of the social, the cultural, the real as they allow or disable modalities of subjects and subjectivities. And this, I would argue, needs to be done under the sign of Foucault's injunction to wake up to the heavy materiality of discourse.[3]

In reconceptualizing the interconnections of sexuality, culture, sociality, discourse, and materiality constituting outside subjects, I return to the question of governmentality as a problematic that brings together a conceptualization of the workings of discourse, disciplines, power, and the formations of subjects and processes of subjectification. Given some of the examples that I have cited, this seems especially pressing at the present time. As Nikolas Rose and Peter Miller put it in a recent article, "The political vocabulary structured by oppositions between state and civil society, public and private, government and the market...does not adequately characterise the diverse ways in which rule is exercised" (1992: 174). And to repeat myself, the terms trotted out to oppose queer theory attest both to a paucity of vocabulary and to a limited vision of the actual state of the social. To take but one instance, the use of *cooption* reveals a vision of the social predicated on the idea that there is a pure, untainted, and discrete position within life or theory. But surely it is clear that "political power is exercised today through a profusion of shifting alliances between diverse authorities in projects to govern a multitude of facets of economic activity, social life and individual conduct" (Rose and Miller, 1992: 174).

Moreover, it is increasingly evident that "power is not so much a matter of imposing constraints upon citizens as of 'making up' citizens capable of bearing a certain kind of regulated freedom" (Rose and Miller, 1992: 174). And yes, power is local, but it is local and localized in, say, the way architectural practices are local: "Architecture embodies certain relations between time, space, functions and persons—the separation of eating and sleeping, for example, or the hierarchical and lateral relations of the enterprise—not only materializing programmatic aspirations but structuring the lives of those caught up in particular architectural regimes" (Rose and Miller, 1992: 184). This vision of power then certainly cannot be said to render the local somehow pristine and abstracted from global, transnational, or a-national structures; if anything, it goes some way in showing that the localization of power is where it is at its most dirty and messy. Be it in the collapse of the Canadian fishing industry and the liquidation of maritime fishing villages, in the Ontario towns emptied by free trade, or in the way that American

AIDS medical and academic discourses are devastating British activists' attempts to promote *safer* sex within a context of HIV-positive rather than AIDS bodies (Watney, 1993), the local is where the global is at its most immediate. This is not to say that the analysis of power inscriptions and movements can be conducted exclusively at a local level; it is to say that postmodern modalities of governmentality produce local exteriorized sites of the a-national, the local transnation or the postnation (Appadurai, 1993). The local and the global simply can no longer be separated from one another; as Hall argues, "The strengthening of 'the local' is probably less the revival of the stable identities of 'locally settled communities' of the past, and more that tricky version of 'the local' which operates within, and has been thoroughly reshaped by 'the global' and operates largely within its logic" (1993: 354). Thinking about these interrelations today then requires analytics capable of grasping the different tensions between space and time that produce qualitatively different modes of subjectification as well as quantitatively new arrangements of populations. This is to recognize the local not as somehow hidden away in interior nooks and crannies but as continually deployed as an outside term—a theme, for instance, that the right successfully employs when it mobilizes an ensemble of technologies of censure on the basis of what an imaginary local community would supposedly support. Arjun Appadurai aptly characterizes America as a series of local outsides, "a postnational space marked by its whiteness but marked too by its uneasy engagement with diasporic peoples, mobile technologies, and queer nationalities" (1993: 412).

The coexistence of several registers is evident here. To respond to these diverse levels, Rose and Miller propose the concept of "translation" in order to designate the processes that translate between and among those entities that we so crudely call "local," "global," "social," or "cultural." Translation refers to both the ways in which "relations are established between the nature, character and causes of problems facing various individuals and groups...so that the problems of the one and those of another seem to be intrinsically linked in their basis and in their solution" and the more literal sense of moving across, "of moving from one person, place or condition to another" (1992: 184). It is in this way that "particular and local issues thus become tied to much larger ones." Lest there be any misapprehension here, this is not a master logic but a rhizomatic fashioning of knowledges that are inscribed at a local level, a local that is never self-sufficient either theoretically or in practice but that is produced out of "'knowledge"—that "vast assemblage of persons, theories, projects, experiments and techniques…from philosophy to medicine" (Rose and Miller, 1992: 177).

Here I return to the subject of the outside of the work of cultural theory and to the ways in which we must work in order to render objects of study as outside, placed at the threshold, the interface, the moment of assemblage and translation between the social, the sexual, the economic, the cultural, etc. While disciplines and agencies produce entities to be governed and managed, the lines of production and management of these spheres always intertwine and overlap. As Donzelot puts it, this is to remember that any division between, for example, the social and the economic has been historically "purely expositional, for 'economic' problems were to be solved by 'social' means…and 'social' problems were to be solved 'economically'" (cited in Rose and Miller, 1992: 205).

In considering the articulations between the different objects of study that are produced in the assemblages and the flanges of governmentality, we are brought to examine the ways in which sexual subjects are produced in the translation of, in the movement across, problems and problematics from one object to another. As Patton argues, we need to "view notions of the social, political, and cultural as descriptions of governmentality, forms of constituting or evading subject positions in relation to the apparatus of the modern state" (1993: 171). Through sexual, social, and cultural practices, we are constantly produced as outside subjects; in Toni Negri's words, "The subject is the limit of a continuous movement between the inside and the outside" (cited in Deleuze, 1990: 238). One way of imagining this movement can be seen in Deleuze's weird little design entitled the "diagram de Foucault," a sort of rough sketch of the way in which the outside is constituted. It is labeled "1. the line of the outside," under which is "2. strategic zones," then "3. strata," and "4. the fold (the zone of subjectification)" (1986: 128). In graphic terms, it depicts the centrality of the fold which rearticulates strategies and historical strata upon the surface, upon the outside. For Deleuze, that fold is itself the movement of the line of social force entailed in and constitutive of new modes of subjectification—of individuals and collectivities.[4]

On the Outside

Beyond internecine battles, I want to locate queer feminist cultural studies as squarely part of the outside and as directed to the outside. In prosaic terms, this is to conceive of theorizing as walking on the Möbius surface of postmodern governmentality's assemblages as they display their goods; produce objects; and enable or disable individuals from forming ties, becoming events. Being on the outside, we are continually in contact with outsiders, agents, and agencies demanding accountability, strangers who become friends, friends who become strangers.

Concomitant with the need to translate among these figures is a certain modesty that entails giving up "the illusion that you can cover, in the textuality of the critical debate, the whole of the world, not recognizing the worldliness of the object you are trying to analyze and place theoretically" (Hall, 1992: 288). And let's be clear about it, the "worldliness" of the object is not a claim for total theory—that sense of the word is heard more clearly in statements about the "social totality" as the requisite object of study. Rather, "worldliness" is produced and reproduced through sustained attempts to make modes of theorizing touch and be touched, touch off movement along the particular lines of governmentality in which we find ourselves. It is produced out of the lateral pressure of surfaces, to make the object, that makes the object, come out differently: as Hall keenly puts it, "I think it is different when you genuinely feel the pressure on our language, to show its workings, to open itself to accessibility" (1992: 289).

If in Hall's injunction to feel the pressure of the social upon our language we have already moved from an individualized situation, it is perhaps unfortunate that the term *translation* tends to return us to the notion of an individual, the intellectual as translator. This sense is obviously incompatible with the epistemological and political challenge of the outside. While the vexing questions of the relationship of theory to practice, individuals to politics, must be continually raised and asked in local ways, one could do worse than remember Foucault and Deleuze's exchange on the question of "intellectuals and power" (Foucault and Deleuze, 1980). Deleuze captures the relation of thought to political activities in the image of a relay: "Practice is an ensemble of relays from one theoretical point to another, and theory, a relay from one practice to another" (Foucault and Deleuze, 1980: 3). Committed to the milieu, one's analyses open onto the necessity for others within the milieu to operate a relay which then leads to another point. And it should be clear that the theorist does not set forward propositions which are in turn acted upon; instead, it is the pressure of the relays themselves— the connections enacted—that formulates for a time the contours of the outside: "the system of relays within an ensemble, in a multiplicity of bits and pieces at once theoretical and practical" (Foucault and Deleuze, 1980: 4). As a bit within the mobile of governmentality, the theorist or writer "has ceased to be a subject, a representing or representative conscience…there is only action, the action of theory, the action of practice within the relations of relays and networks" (Foucault and Deleuze, 1980: 4).

In small ways, and even beyond the more obvious pressure of the pedagogic surface, like many I participate in this relay race in very quotidian ways. For instance, given the particular outside that I inhabit, I am often called upon by various forms of media to "explain" some facet of the surface that is Québécois life at the moment. They are mostly subjects that some might find trivial, ranging from body piercing, the success of talk shows, the phenomenon of current *téléromans* to latchkey kids, a sociological explanation of blue jeans, homophobia and violence, the "sandwich" generation, the question of gay and lesbian cultures, and the burning of bras in France. And the forums are varied: traditional women's magazines, newspapers, student associations, fashion mags, very commercial tv, state-run television, local cable channels, student radio, etc. When I don't know anything about the subject I pass it on to someone else, who may have previously passed a subject on to me. When I respond, I do so with a program in mind and in practice. I tread a rhizomatic if not twisted line: as my neighbor put it, kidding me about one such performance, "How did you get from her question of *Les filles de Caleb* to questions of gay and lesbian rights, the role of sexuality in Québec's past, immigration, and being out as a lesbian in the university?"

Again, this is but one local example, in part produced by the fact that sociology has a lingering, if waning, importance in the Québécois everyday that as a discipline it no longer has elsewhere, and in part due to the closer relations of proximity between universities, the media, and other governmental nodes within the smallness of Québec society. However, as the recent Québec Human Rights hearings on discrimination against gays and lesbians demonstrated, there is a demand on the part of other parts of the current assemblage of governmentality for help. And this is not some nasty form of cooption; it is more often than not a seemingly sincere demand for us to open out our language. It is for me yet another example of the rearranged relations of proximity among agents and agencies. As one commissioner said, "Give us a sociological framework in which to rethink the connections of gays and lesbians, the family, and Québec society." It was a question asked in urgency and with feeling, and as the official sociologist of the group to whom the question was posed, I gave a surface to some of the arguments that I have pursued in the course of this book.[5] This is not to say that it was a superficial version of some deep argument because they wouldn't be able to comprehend the import of our profound thinking. Nor is to say that we compromised ourselves and gave them what they wanted to hear. Rather, it was another small attempt to go with the pressure bearing on language and comportment to turn inside out, to splay thoughts, a modest acknowledgment of the need to translate and connect various objects. And rather than seeing this as being helplessly drawn within the internal workings of government, I see this as necessarily being part and parcel of the outside, modes of translation and movement across the processes of postmodern governmentality, a recognition that "the theories of the social sciences, of economics, of sociology and of psychology, thus provide a kind of *intellectual machinery* for government, in the form of procedures for rendering the world thinkable" (Rose and Miller, 1992: 182).

This description compels a reordering of how we go about theorizing and placing queer feminist cultural studies. If the theories mobilized in current governmentality have so far tended toward quantitative calibrations, this is but a further challenge to those of us who deal in the words and the images, the sounds and the sights of the social. At the same time, it strikes me as drastically insufficient to think that we can merrily go along with a notion of queer cultural studies that takes sexuality as its object as it vaguely gestures to "the social," "the political." And while it may be genial, and may even have been at one time necessary to define "queer" as marking "a flexible space for the expression of all aspects non- (anti-, contra-) straight cultural production and reception" (Doty, 1993: 3), this is now both radically too much and way too little.

Against versions of "cultural insiderism," the outside of queer feminist cultural studies takes as an *a priori* point that "identity discourse is a strategy in a field of power in which the so-called identity movements attempt to alter the conditions for constituting the political subject" (Patton, 1993: 145). Conceptualizing and putting this political subject to work is deadly serious, even as it may be done through the analysis of cultural practices, some of which may indeed be fun. Following Grosz, this is a call for a program that

> rethink[s] the relations between the social and the subjective so they are no longer seen as polar opposites; rethinking all the productions of the 'mind'—theory, knowledge, art, cultural practices...and notions of agency and political action in terms of micro-processes, thousands of sub-struggles and proliferating the field of politics so that it encompasses the entire social field. (1993: 68–69)

A Parting Desire

As a conclusion that seeks to open rather than close, I end with a call to outside ourselves, to render and to surface thoughts, actions, feelings, wishes as a program of study, the program that produces us, so that we can in turn engage different modes of intervening in the social through various forms of theoretical work. As I have tried to argue across the essays in this book, if the stakes are high, there is no one way to go about this. That said, what I have tried to argue here is for another mode of getting about, of being transported by vectors of desire that refigure traditional lines of division between the social, the sexual, the real, the cultural, the national, the theoretical. If I have privileged the concepts of the outside and the surface, it is because they allow for a vision of the interconnections between these supposedly discrete entities. I am profoundly convinced that they reveal something of the ways in which the social field is actually ordered and lived. This glimpse of the social arranged on the surface is, of course, not sufficient unto itself; rather, the view from the outside challenges me to consider how virtual relations of proximity between individuals and collectivities may be actualized and folded in other ways, encouraged in other directions. If I have argued against the idea of identity, it is because it can only describe the specificities of categories of belonging; it cannot reach the desires to belong and the ways in which individuals, groups, and nations render and live out their specificity as singular: as that which is now, in this way, with this affect. In turn, any singularity of belonging must continually be freed and encouraged in its movement to constantly become other. Being on the outside, we are drawn within the ever moving interweaving of the lines of the social, lines that we render as the surface of sexuality, gender, race, economics, class, etc.: in short, the outside of contemporary sociality, the limits which allow for other ways of conceiving and enacting belonging. We need to be compelled by these desires, these limits, the moving but so-what ways in which aspiration is played out. If I have insisted on some of the everyday manners of being that are lived all around, I also emphasize that our ways of thinking and describing them must be up to the task of rendering the social field vibrant, looking at it and for it in ways that may be more open to experimentation and change.

Across these essays I have tried to embody certain relations of belonging, the desires that move us at different times and in different ways to engage. This engagement is for me at once personal, writerly, social, and political. Fundamentally, it is an engagement with where I live and how I wish to be able to live. A wish that is for alternative relations of sociality, of thought, of friendship, of practice, of succor. If I write from a singular milieu, I also have a theoretical *parti pris*. While the theoretical perspectives I draw upon are important, of more import is the way in which they are put to work together. In other words, while I could enumerate the different strands (obviously with Foucault and Deleuze in the forefront along with feminist reversionings), it is more crucial to consider how theories, fiction and fictions, and discursive examples (be they films, television shows, government statements, or seized snippets of conversation) commingle, their surfaces rubbing each other as they produce a momentary but richly interwoven outside. I am in turn committed to this outside, a commitment that I hope does not aggrandize the singularities which form me. For what I have tried to experiment with here is the wager that in writing we become-other, becoming that of which we write and think. While there are no assurances that this will play out in immediate ways, that the social will be miraculously rearranged, listening more carefully, looking more acutely—in short, being deeply interested in life—may help to renew the energy we need now and in the future if we are to encourage relations of belonging that peacefully and joyously coexist.

Elspeth Probyn

Once more, I go back to the summer streets of Montréal, to the ways in which individuals driven from the interior of their homes, of their political belonging, are thrust together on the surface of the city. While it is not sufficient to merely state that this outside produces some very weird translations between and among individuals carried along by lines of culture, sexuality, social modalities, and political intentions, it is, I think, instructive to take this assemblage to heart; to place it at the heart of our studies, one that does not beat hidden inside the body of theory but that is displayed, that constitutes our social skins—the outside of our belongings.

postscript

It is the very end of October, and from my desk I look out at palm trees and morning glories. I sit waiting for friends to phone with news of the Québec referendum, wondering whether the land that I have left will become sovereign. Finally I hear of the uncomfortable results—defeated by less than 1 percent, Québec is for the moment still with Canada. My friends tell me that it is snowing. Here on the other side of the gray approach of winter, it is that strange period just after Daylight Savings Time has begun when people wander around slightly dazed by light where before there was darkness. I clumsily navigate the myriad of mundane difficulties entailed by immigrating, struck by the incommensurability of everyday life when things don't mean or work quite the same. Questions of belonging hover and are pushed to the side in favor of more immediate preoccupations: learning to ride a motorbike, looking for a place to live. Of course the insecurities rush in: as at low tide, doubts are littered across the surface of a new life. Taking liberties with the organization of things, overstepping the bounds of proper behavior, space, and hemisphere, it seems so presumptuous to move to the other side of the world, a leap of faith sustained on hope.

I had thought that the rigors of departure—the forms filled out, blood taken for tests, tears pushed to the furthest recesses—would have hardened me for the impact of arrival. But I am brought up short by the sudden jolt of what it means to be inbetween two countries. "Qu'est-ce que j'ai fait?" I asked myself over and over during the first few days. The rawness of new sights, objects, and manners of being pervades, and I ache from the constant registering of degrees of proximity and difference between countries and people. Skin is momentarily unequal to the task, and impressions are directly communicated to my guts: no mediation here, *les tripes* as research protocol.

Slowly the brutality of intensity wanes, allowing me to consider the *umheimlich* decision to move from one culture in which I had embedded myself to another that is both totally foreign and disconcerting in its familiarity—I think I remember some things, but they are misleading bits from another time, another place: a sort of cultural false-memory syndrome.

And so the search for singularity recommences even as I am astride countries and cultures. At first I wondered whether it was ironic that having written a book on belonging, I should uproot myself. On reflection, it is quite normal that in the process of writing I have become-other, that my thinking about belonging has coincided with a transversal move which radically disturbs any complacency and rudely reminds me of the rigors of the outside. But it is an outside matted with rhizomatic roots, and thoughts and desires once again begin to grow. Having mercilessly worried about the concepts of singularity, desire, and belonging on the outside, what I wish to produce now seems so evident: a moment when desire comes together with the full sensation of what is possible at this time, in this place, with these people, things, and ideas.

Sydney, November 1995

notes

Introduction

1 As will be clear, I am deeply indebted to Grosz's work. In fact, I vaguely recall our first meeting many years ago when, walking and talking through the snowy streets of Toronto, it dawned on me that the book I had just finished was more about desire than its overt subject, the self.

Chapter 1

1 I am playing a bit fast and loose here, as Hannah's argument proposes that "the specificity of a discursive formation implies not only its uniqueness and its 'exclusive actuality,' but also its 'could not have been otherwise'" (Hannah, 1993: 356). In *Foucault* (1986), Deleuze refers precisely to this as singularity. For an exhaustive explication of singularity within the vocabulary of Deleuze and Guattari, see Brain Massumi (1992), who places Agamben as a post-Deleuzian.

2 These may sound like trivial activities, but being displaced to southern California reminded me of their importance as I faced that emptiness when, at the end of the day, everyone disappears into their cars and far-flung houses, leaving the streets barren.

On a more important note, for those outside of Québec, it may seem strange that I designate Québec as postcolonial. Granted, it is a less clear-cut situation than, say, that of Cameroon, yet it is firmly how French Québec thinks of itself. And when one considers that, for instance, twenty years ago it was impossible to enter postsecondary studies without going through "*le collège classique*," the Catholic program administered directly from France, or that the federal government in Ottawa had tanks rolling down the main streets of Montréal through the imposition of the War Measures Act, postcolonialism is a part of the Québécois social imaginary that is fairly easy to understand.

Chapter 2

1 My thanks to Shulamit Lechtman for this image.

2 In any case, there are many much better placed than I to do this. For

instance, see Grosz (1994a; 1994b), Fuss (1991), Braidotti (1992), de Lauretis (1994), and Butler (1993).

3 See also Paul Patton's (1995) use of Deleuze and Guattari within the realm of political philosophy. Taking up the way that "Deleuze's social theory always recognised the primacy of those transformative moments in which societies pass from one form of organisation or capture to another," Patton opens the way for an alternative and more informative analysis of the pressing question of indigenous land claims in colonial and postcolonial societies.

4 Given my previous interest in anorexia nervosa, I obviously am not suggesting that we ignore the ways in which this experimentation with bodies and images is channelled in sometimes fatal directions. Indeed, we must continue to focus on the ways in which young girls' bodies as potentially open lines of flight are closed down in quite often tragic ways.

5 The performance artist Suzanne Westenhoefer captures this perfectly in her monologue about her desire for Martina Navratalova, a desire not for the whole of Martina but expressed as an overwhelming longing to lick the coursing vein that pops out on the inside of Martina's forearm. This image, in turn, may connect and relate with others: her butchness, her accent, her skill, her physicality, her success. All these images are displayed and arranged in the relation of bodies and parts that we call so familiarly "Martina," a machinic entity that spectacularly engages squads of lesbian fans.

Chapter 3

1 The two French terms used to signify supposedly "original" Québécois are "*de souche*" ("old stock," "of the source") and "*pure laine*" ("pure wool"). In terms of geography, Montréal is regarded by hard nationalists as the least *pure laine* place in the province because of its lingering Anglophone facade and its greater concentration of immigrants.

2 As one can imagine, the reactions to Parizeau's statement were varied. My favorite line from the debates that ensued was Parizeau's rather exasperated response as to what "*de souche*" Québécois were to call themselves: "After all, they don't want us to call ourselves '*les tabernacos*.'" *Los tabernacos* is the derogatory term for Québécois vacationing in Mexico. It stems from the Québec swear word "*tabernac*." Like much Québécois profanity, "tabernacle" comes from the Church. Michel Tremblay's recent novel includes a wonderful, if

rather cruel, short story about two complaining couples in Mexico, aptly entitled "Los Tabernacos" (Tremblay, 1993).

3 Within the Australian context, vigorous critiques have focused on the ways in which multiculturalism as a concept is wedded to that of tolerance. As Ghassan Hage argues in his article "Locating Multiculturalism's Other: A Critique of Practical Tolerance" (1994), tolerance plays out as a game of power between the majority community and its others.

For an acerbic account of the debates on multiculturalism in Canada, see Neil Bissoondath's book *Selling Illusions: The Cult of Multiculturalism in Canada* (1994).

4 In a slightly different theoretical project to which I am nonetheless indebted, Martin Allor (1993) argues that Lefebvre, along with other nationalist cultural producers, articulates a "vision of pastoral left-nationalism" through the key trope of "le métissage."

5 For one of the best evocations of Innis's work with regard to a nostalgic Canadian imaginary, see Arthur Kroker, *Technology and the Canadian Mind: Innis/McLuhan/Grant* (1984). See also Jody Berland's work on Innis, communication technologies, and space (1992). James Carey's work (1989; 1975) has been of great importance in introducing Innis to American communications scholars, thus posthumously reducing some of Innis's isolation and perhaps making Canadian inissian theorists feel less marginal.

In speaking of Innis, I have in mind *Empire and Communication* (1972) and *The Bias of Communication*, in particular the essay "Minerva's Owl" (1951).

6 On "*sexe et genre*," see Hurtig, Kail, and Rouch (1991), Delphy (1991); and Mathieu (1989). In North America, Francophone Québec feminists are quite unique in their appropriation of French materialist feminism. Danielle Juteau and Nicole Laurin (1989) provide a clear positioning of the concepts of French materialist feminism. See also a collection of Guillaumin's translated essays with an introduction by Juteau (1995).

7 My thanks to Line Grenier for suggesting Vigneault's song in this context.

8 Over its twenty-week season, the supermarkets were empty, the streets lonely as nearly half of the Francophone population (some 3 million) stayed home to watch, to which one can add the scores of readers who bought the best-selling novel by Arlette Cousture from which it was adapted. For a compelling analysis of the specifically Québécois nature of the genre of *téléroman*, see Saint-Jacques and de la Garde (1992).

9 The sequel *Blanche* was in many ways more interesting than *Les filles*. It takes up the story with Blanche, the eldest of Emilie's daughters, who becomes a nurse in Abitibi after having endured the humiliation of being refused entrance to McGill's Medical Faculty, a refusal explicitly framed as a rejection of her both as a woman and as a French-Canadian. The scabrous husband returns to lurk, but very much in a backstage manner.

10 *Vide* Pierre Eliott Trudeau—as "P.E.T.," the "playboy prime minister"— argued that "the State has no business in the bedrooms of the nation" as he did his best to render the public image of Canada somewhat more sexy.

11 On the ways in which Montréal operated discursively as the figure of sex and vice in the English-Canadian imaginary, especially in the '40s and '50s, see Will Straw's fascinating article (1992).

12 My thanks to my colleague Jacques Brazeau for this apparently well-known image. In *Montréal, P.Q.*, the adopted son of the principal madam is sent off to a seminary. He leaves with a garter belt, and, in a wonderfully baroque scene, this young man "in a dress" masturbates with it. (We are shown that he is having a very wet dream.) An older priest catches him at it and sympathetically takes him off for a dip in a cold lake.

13 While I haven't the time to do justice to Schwartzwald's extremely important argument, which has directly inspired my own, I direct the reader to his article (1991) and to a recently translated one (1993).

14 In case one thinks that homosociality is the sole prerogative of men, in this scene Arcand endeavors to represent a female homosocial space as relations between women are set up through the objectified body of one man. Obviously, it is impossible for female homosociality to attain the status and power of that of male homosociality, and Arcand's attempt can be read either as reactive whining or as liberal good intentions (or both).

15 Intriguingly enough, Arcand's latest film, *Love and Human Remains*, is based on a play by Brad Fraser, a hip, queer, generation-x Canadian playwright. The diegesis, which is originally set in Edmonton but gets moved to Montréal in Arcand's version, revolves around a single gay guy who eventually falls in love.

16 In an early article on lesbians and gays in Québécois cinema, Tom Waugh also cites Arcand and goes on to demonstrate that while the figure of the homosexual has been prevalent, most of the representations have also been homophobic. Waugh's article provides an insightful contextualization of

the history of gay and lesbian representations within Québécois cinema of the '60s and '70s (Waugh, 1980). See also Nadeau's positioning of the films of Léa Pool in regard to the impossibility of lesbian filmic representation (1992; 1993).

17 *Parler pour parler* has since been replaced by a new show, *Janette tout court*. Janette continues her odyssey into Québécois sexual manners in an episode where she investigates what she called "s/m made in Québec."

18 As soon as Jacques Parizeau did indeed become the new premier of Québec, one of his first statements was that it was time to make "Québec into a normal country."

19 As a final note, long after I had finished writing this essay, the Québec referendum on sovereignty failed by a mere 50,000 votes (or less than 1 percent). Jacques Parizeau disgraced himself by blaming the defeat on Anglophone moneyed interests and the ethnic vote. He resigned without apologizing.

Chapter 4

1 The exact wording of Chapter 1.1, Article 10, is as follows: "Everyone has the right to the recognition and exercise, in full equality, of the rights and liberties of the person, without distinction, exclusion or preference founded on race, color, sex, pregnancy, sexual orientation, civil status, age except in measures set out by law, religion, political conviction, language, ethnic or national origin, social condition, handicap or the use of a means to overcome this handicap." The trouble comes later when in Article 137 sexual orientation disappears as a valid reason for contesting exclusion or discrimination before any social benefits regime, be it private or state funded.

   For the record, I do not think that the issue of conjugal rights for same-sex partners is by any means the most important stake in the current legal contestations. It is important only insofar as the legal definition of the family is restructured to include various forms of affective relationships.

2 In Lucy Maud Montgomery's classic story, the "unconventional" Anne is adopted by an elderly sibling couple. With respect to the brief submitted on conjugal rights, Boyd's was a welcome intervention in that we (Gloria Escomel, Lise Harou, Nicole Lacelle, and I) sought to point out that, say, two sisters who had lived together all their lives should be eligible to share in each other's retirement benefits. Boyd, however, did not expand on the

numerous and highly meditated girlfriend rituals that the tomboy Anne initiates with her "bosom friend" Diana.

3 My thanks to Judith Halberstam for reminding me of this point. While obviously key to this argument about gender and queer childhood, the work of deconstructing the binarism of gender, especially in regard to transexuality,is beyond the scope of my essay. However, I refer the reader to Halberstam's work on female masculinity (1994), Sandy Stone's on post-transsexuality (1992), and Ki Namaste's on the position of transsexuality within queer theory (1994). If the epistemological basis of these quantitative studies is inadequate to the study of gender identification and homosexuality, the question of transsexuality is totally beyond their ken. However, as Namaste argues, queer theory itself has so far proven to be less than illuminating on this point.

4 In a beautiful visual project, Martha Townsend's site-responsive installation *La chasse galérie* replays the magic and the material, national, and gender specificity of this tale (Strokestown, Ireland, 1989).

Chapter 5

1 Having dealt with a fair amount of criticism that my work is overly theoretical, it should be clear that I am not encouraging a strain of anti-intellectualism that surfaces in some feminist critiques. The outside is also a challenge to nontheory types to read a little closer, just as it is for me to write less densely (this essay being the exception to the rule).

2 Morton does explicitly recognize the polemical nature of his text, and in a footnote that flags one of the pretextual conditions of its publication, he states that the essay was turned down by *Critical Inquiry* "on the grounds that it 'personalizes,' becomes 'polemical,'" against which Morton defends himself by arguing that "the scholarly/polemical binary is itself maintained by the very people who are maintaining dominant academic power relations; they need the term 'polemic' to get rid of that scholarship not in their class interests" (1993: 143 fn).

3 It does strikes me as astonishing that over ten years after his death so many Anglo-American theorists can continue to run on strange readings of Foucault's theory: that discourse has replaced materiality; that power is rendered vapid; that he was a rampant individualist; etc. Of course, readings are influenced by the disciplinary and geopolitical space in which Foucault

is read. Thus, it is notable that feminist and queer cultural geographers, many theorists in the humanities in Australia, and several of my Canadian colleagues produce foucauldian-inspired social theory that has little to do with the ways in which Foucault has been taken up and/or put down in American literature departments.

4 Elsewhere (1992; 1993), I have given a more exhaustive account of Deleuze's reading of Foucault through the use of the figure of the fold (*le pli*).

5 The members of the group presenting the brief were Gloria Escomel, Lise Harou, Nicole Lacelle, and I. I thank them for including me in this relay race, the point of which was an argument for other forms of familial sociality.

bibliography

Agamben, Giorgio. (1993) "Forme-de-vie." *Futur antérieur*, 15, pp. 81–85.

————. (1990)*La communauté qui vient: Une théorie de la singularité quelconque*. Paris: Seuil. Translated by Michael Hardt, *The Coming Community*. Minneapolis: University of Minnesota Press, 1993.

————. (1989) *Enfance et histoire: Dépérissement de l'expérience et origine de l'histoire*. Translated by Yves Hersant. Paris: Éditions Payot.

————. (1987) "The Thing Itself." *Substance*, 16:53, pp. 18–28.

Alliez, Eric. (1993) *La signature du monde, ou qu'est-ce que la philosophie de Deleuze et Guattari*. Paris: Les éditions du Cerf.

Allor, Martin. (1993) "Cultural Métissage: National Formations and Productive Discourses in Québec Cinema and Television." *Screen*, 34:1, pp. 65–70.

Anderson, Benedict. (1983) *Imagined Communities: Reflections on the Origin and Spread of Nationalism*. London: Verso.

Anshaw, Carol. (1993) *Aquamarine*. London: Virago.

Anzaldúa, Gloria. (1991) "To(o) Queer the Writer—Loca, escritora y chicana." In Betsy Warland (ed.), *InVersions: Writing by Dykes, Queers and Lesbians*. Vancouver: Press Gang Publishers.

————. (1990) "She Ate Horses." In Jeffner Allen (ed.), *Lesbian Philosophies and Cultures*. Albany: SUNY Press.

Appadurai, Arjun. (1993) "Patriotism and Its Futures." *Public Culture*, 5:3, pp. 411–430.

Arthur, Kateryna Olijnyk. (1988) "Between Literatures: Canada and Australia," *Ariel*, 19:1, pp. 3–12.

Bailey, Michael J., Joseph S. Miller, and Lee Wilierman. (1993) "Maternally Rated Childhood Gender Nonconformity in Homosexuals and Heterosexuals." *Archives of Sexual Behavior*, 22, 461–469.

Barthes, Roland. (1977) *Image-Music-Text*. Translated by Stephen Heath. New York: Hill and Wang.

Baudrillard, Jean. *A l'ombre des majorités silencieuses ou la fin du social*. Paris: Denoel/Gonthier.

Bell, David, Jon Binnie, Julia Cream, and Gill Valentine. (1994) "All Hyped

Up and No Place to Go." *Gender, Place and Culture*, 1, pp. 31–47.

Bellour, Raymond. (1989) "Vers la fiction." In *Michel Foucault: Philosophe*. Paris: Seuil, pp. 172–181.

————. (1977) "Hitchcock, The Enunciator." *Camera Obscura*, 2, pp. 69–94.

Bergson, Henri. (1990 [1959]) *Matière et mémoire*. Paris: Quadrige/PUF.

Berland, Jody. (1992) "Angels Dancing: Cultural Technologies and the Production of Space." In L. Grossberg, C. Nelson, and P. Treichler (eds.), *Cultural Studies*. London and New York: Routledge.

Berlant, Lauren. (1995) "1968, Or the Revolution of the Little Queers." In Diane Elam and Robyn Wiegman (eds.), *Feminism Beside Itself*. New York and London: Routledge.

Berthelot, Jean Michel. (1992) "Du corps comme opérateur discursif ou les apories d'une sociologie du corps." *Sociologies et sociétés*, 24:1, pp. 10–18.

Bhabha, Homi K. (1994) *The Location of Culture*. New York and London: Routledge.

Birtha, Becky. (1993) "Jonnieruth." In Bennett L. Singer (ed.), *Growing Up Gay*. New York: New Press, pp. 18–22.

Bissoondath, Neil. (1994) *Selling Illusions: The Cult of Multiculturalism in Canada*. Harmondsworth: Penguin.

Bland, Lucy, and Frank Mort. (1984) "Look Out for the 'Good Time Girl': Dangerous Sexualities as Threat to National Health." *Formations of Nations and People*. London: RKP.

Braidotti, Rosi. (1991) *Patterns of Dissonance*. Cambridge: Polity.

————. (1989) "The Politics of Ontological Difference." In Teresa Brennan (ed.), *Between Feminism and Psychoanalysis*. New York: Routledge, pp. 89–105.

Brossard, Nicole. (1991) "Green Night of Labyrinth Park." In Betsy Warland (ed.), *InVersions: Writing by Dykes, Queers and Lesbians*. Vancouver: Press Gang Publishers.

Brunt, Rosalind. (1989) "The Politics of Identity." In Stuart Hall and Martin Jacques (eds.), *New Times: The Changing Face of Politics in the 1990s*. London: Lawrence & Wishart.

Butler, Judith. (1993) *Bodies That Matter*. New York and London: Routledge.

Carey, James. (1989) *Communication as Culture: Essays on Media and Society*. Boston: Unwin and Hyman.

————. (1975) "Canadian Communication Theory." In G. Robinson and D. Theall (eds.), *Studies in Canadian Communication*. Montréal: McGill University.

Colette. (1971) *The Pure and the Impure*. Translated by Herma Briffault. Harmondsworth: Penguin.

Commission des droits de la personne. (1994) *De l'illégalité a l'équalité*. Les publications du Québec.

Crimp, Douglas. (1992) "Portraits of People with AIDS." In Lawrence Grossberg, Cary Nelson, and Paula Treichler (eds.), *Cultural Studies*. London and New York: Routledge.

Davis, Fred. (1979) *Yearning for Yesterday: A Sociology of Nostalgia*. New York: Free Press.

de Lauretis, Teresa. (1994) *The Practice of Love: Lesbian Sexuality and Perverse Desire*. Bloomington: Indiana University Press.

———. (1991) "The Film and the Visible." In Bad Object-Choices (eds.), *How Do I Look? Queer Film and Video*. Seattle: Bay Press.

———. (1988) "Sexual Indifference and Lesbian Representation." *Theatre Journal*, 40:2, pp. 155–177.

Deleuze, Gilles. (1994) "Désir et plaisir." *Le magazine littéraire*, 325 (October), pp. 59–65.

———. (1993) *Critique et clinique*. Paris: Les éditions de minuit.

———. (1992) "Ethology: Spinoza and Us." in Jonathan Crary and Sanford Kwinter (eds.), *Incorporations*. New York: Zone Books.

———. (1991) *Bergsonism*. Translated by Hugh Tomlinson and Barbara Habberjam. New York: Zone Books.

———. (1990) *Pourparlers*. Paris: Les éditions de minuit.

———. (1990) (interview by Toni Negri) "Le devenir révolutionnaire et les créations politiques." *Futur Antérieur*, 1, pp. 100–108.

———. (1989) "Qu'est-ce qu'un dispositif?" In *Michel Foucault: Philosophe*. Paris: Seuil.

———. (1986) *Foucault*. Paris: Les éditions de minuit.

———. (1979) "Foreword: The Rise of the Social." In Jacques Donzelot (ed.), *The Policing of Families*. New York: Pantheon Books.

Delphy, Christine. (1993) "Rethinking Sex and Gender." *Women's Studies International Forum*, 16:11, pp. 1–9.

———. (1991) "Penser le genre: Quels problèmes?" In Marie-Claude Hurtig, Michèle Kail, and Hélène Rouch (eds.), *Sexe et genre: De la hiérarchie entre les sexes*. Paris: CNRS.

Donzelot, Jacques. (1993) "The Invention of the Social." In M. Gane and T.

Johnson (eds.), *Foucault's New Domains*. London and New York: Routledge.

Doty, Alexander. (1993) *Making Things Perfectly Queer: Interpreting Mass Culture*. Minneapolis: University of Minnesota Press.

Dyer, Richard. (1994) "The Light of the World." Paper presented at The Body of Gender Conference, Offenes Kulturhaus, Linz, Austria.

Eliot, T. S. (1963) "The Journey of the Magi." *The Wasteland and Other Poems*. London and Boston: Faber and Faber.

Foucault, Michel. (1994 [1963]) "Distance, aspect, origine." In Daniel Defert and François Éwald (eds.), *Dits et écrits*. Vol. 1. Paris: Gallimard, pp. 272–285.

———. (1992 [1963]) *Raymond Roussel*. Paris: Folio.

———. (1989) *Foucault Live*. New York: Semiotext(e).

———. (1987) "Maurice Blanchot: The Thought from the Outside." *Foucault/Blanchot*. Translated by Brian Massumi. New York: Zone Books.

———. (1986) "Of Other Spaces." *Diacritics*, pp. 22–27.

———. (1985) "Archéologie d'une passion." *Magazine littéraire*, 221, pp. 100–105.

———. (1984a) "An Interview: Sex, Power and the Politics of Identity" (with Bob Gallagher and Alexander Wilson). *The Advocate*, 44 (August).

———. (1984b) "Polemics, Politics, and Problematizations: An Interview with Michel Foucault." In Paul Rabinow (ed.), *The Foucault Reader*. New York: Pantheon Books.

———. (1982) "La pensée, l'émotion." *Duane Michals Photographies de 1958–1982*. Paris: Editions du Musée d'Art Moderne. Reprinted in *Dits et écrits*. Paris: Gallimard, 1994.

———. (1980) "Questions on Geography." In Colin Gordon (ed.), *Power/Knowledge*. Translated by C. Gordon, L. Marshall, J. Mepham, and K. Soper. New York: Pantheon.

——— and Gilles Deleuze. (1980) "Entretien: Les Intellectuels et le pouvoir." *L'Arc*, 49, pp. 3–10.

———. (1977) "Nietzsche, Genealogy, History." *Language, Counter-Memory, Practice*. Translated by Donald F. Bouchard and Sherry Simon. Ithaca: Cornell University Press, pp. 139–164.

——— and Hélène Cixous. (1975) "A Propos de Marguerite Duras." *Cahiers Renaud Barrault*, 89, pp. 8–25.

———. (1993) *The Order of Things*. New York: Vintage Books.

————. (1972) *The Archeology of Knowledge*. New York: Pantheon.

————. (1971) *L'ordre du discours*. Paris: Gallimard.

Frémont, Christiane. (1991) "Complication et singularité." *Revue de Métaphysique et Morale*, 1, pp. 105–120.

Fuss, Diana,169 (ed.), (1991) *Inside/Out. Lesbian Theories, Gay Theories*. New York and London: Routledge.

Galford, Ellen. (1993) *The Dyke and the Dybbuk*. Seattle: Seal Press.

Gatens, Moira. (1994) "Ethological Bodies: Gender as Affect and Power." Paper presented at The Body of Gender Conference, Offenes Kulturhaus, Linz, Austria.

Gilroy, Paul. (1993) *The Black Atlantic: Modernity and Double Consciousness*. Cambridge: Harvard University Press.

Gomez, Jewelle. (1995) "Wink of an Eye." In Catherine E. McKinley and L. DeLaney (eds.), *Afrekete: An Anthology of Black Lesbian Writing*. New York: Doubleday.

Gomez-Peña, Guillermo. (1993) *Warrior for Gringostroika*. Minneapolis: Graywolf Press.

Gordon, Colin. (1991) "Governmental Rationality: An Introduction." In G. Burchell, C. Gordon, and P. Miller (eds.), *The Foucault Effect: Studies in Governmentality*. Chicago: Chicago University Press.

————. (1981) "The Subtracting Machine." *I & C*, 8, pp. 27–40.

————. (1980) "Afterword." In C. Gordon (ed.), *Power/Knowledge*. New York: Pantheon Books.

Gouvernement du Québec. (1976) *La charte des droits de la personne*. Les publications du Québec.

Gross, Larry. (1993) *Contested Closets: The Politics and Ethics of Outing*. Minneapolis: University of Minnesota Press.

Grossberg, Lawrence. (1992) *We Gotta Get Out of This Place: Popular Conservatism and Postmodern Culture*. New York and London: Routledge.

Grosz, Elizabeth. (1995) "Architecture from the Outside." *Space, Time, and Perversion*. New York and London: Routledge.

———— and Elspeth Probyn (eds.), (1995) *Sexy Bodies: The Strange Carnalities of Feminism*. New York and London: Routledge.

————. (1994a) *Volatile Bodies: Toward a Corporeal Feminism*. Bloomington: Indiana University Press.

————. (1994b) "Refiguring Lesbian Desire." In Laura Doan (ed.), *The*

Lesbian Postmodern. New York: Columbia University Press.

————. (1994c) "Theorizing Corporeality: Bodies, Sexuality and the Feminist Academy." *Melbourne Journal of Politics*, 22, pp. 3–29.

————. (1993) "Nietzsche and the Stomach for Knowledge." In Paul Patton (ed.), *Nietzsche, Feminism and Political Theory*. London and New York: Routledge.

Guattari, Félix. (1992) "Regimes, Pathways, Subjects." In Jonathan Crary and Sanford Kwinter (eds.), *Incorporations*. New York: Zone.

Guillaumin, Colette. (1995) *Racism, Sexism, Power and Ideology*. London and New York: Routledge.

————. (1979) "Questions de différence." *Questions féministes*, 6, pp. 3–21.

————. (1978) "Pratique du pouvoir et idée de nature (2): Le discours de la Nature." *Questions féministes*, 3, pp. 5–28.

Hage, Ghassan. (1994) "Locating Multiculturalism's Other: A Critique of Practical Tolerance." *New Formations*, 24, pp. 19–34.

Halberstam, Judith. (1994) "F2M: The Making of Female Masculinity." In Laura Doan (ed.), *The Lesbian Postmodern*. New York: Columbia University Press, pp. 210–228.

Hall, Radclyffe. (1968) *The Well of Loneliness*. London: Corgi Books.

Hall, Stuart. (1993) "Culture, Community, Nation." *Cultural Studies*, 7:3, pp. 349–363.

————. (1992) "Cultural Studies and Its Theoretical Legacies." In L. Grossberg, C. Nelson and P. Treichler (eds.), *Cultural Studies*. London and New York: Routledge.

————. (1986) "On Postmodernism and Articulation: An Interview with Stuart Hall." In Lawrence Grossberg (ed.), *Journal of Communication Inquiry*, 2:2, pp. 91–114.

————. (1985) "Signification, Representation, Ideology: Althusser and the Post-structuralist Debates." *Critical Studies in Mass Communication*, 10:2, pp. 91–114.

————. (1980) "Encoding/Decoding." In S. Hall et al. (eds.), *Culture, Media, Language*. London: Hutchison.

————. (1977) "Culture, Media and the 'Ideological' Effect." In J. Curran et al. (eds.), *Mass Communication and Society*. London: Edward Arnold.

Halperin, David. (1995) *Saint Foucault: Towards a Gay Hagiography*. New York: Oxford University Press.

Hannah, M. (1993) "Foucault on Theorizing Specificity." *Environment and Planning D: Society and Space*, 11, pp. 349–363.

Haraway, Donna. (1985) "A Manifesto for Cyborgs: Science, Technology, and Socialist Feminism in the 1980s." *Socialist Review*, 80.

Heal, Linda. (1993) "It Happened on Main Street." In B.L. Singer (ed.), *Growing Up Gay*. New York: Free Press, pp. 8–14.

Hennessy, Rosemary. (1993) "Queer Theory: A Review of the *Differences* Special Issue and Wittig's *The Straight Mind*," *Signs*, 18:4, pp. 964–973.

Hockenberry, Stewart L., and Robert. E. Billingham. (1987) "Sexual Orientation and Boyhood Gender Conformity: Development of the Boyhood Gender Nonconformity Scale (BGCS)." *Archives of Sexual Behavior,* 16, pp. 475–92.

Hocquenghem, Guy. (1993) *Homosexual Desire*. Translated by Daniella Dangoor. Durham: Duke University Press.

Hoggart, Richard. (1963) "A Question of Tone: Some Problems in Autobiographical Writing." *Critical Quarterly*, 5:1, pp. 73–90.

Hurtig, Marie-Claire, Michèle Kail, and Hélène Rouch (eds.), (1991) *Sexe et genre: De la hiéarchie entre les sexes*. Paris: CNRS.

Hutcheon, Linda. (1988) *The Canadian Postmodern*. Oxford: University of Oxford Press.

Innis, Harold A. (1972) *Empire and Communication*. Toronto: University of Toronto Press.

———. (1951) *The Bias of Communication*. Toronto: University of Toronto Press.

Jagose, Annamarie. (1993) "Way Out: The Category of 'Lesbian' and the Fantasy of the Utopic Space." *Journal of History of Sexuality*, 4:2, pp. 264–287.

Jameson, Fredric. (1983) "Euphorias of Substitution: Hubert Aquin and the Political Novel in Québec." *Yale French Studies*, 65, pp. 214–223.

———. (1979) "Reification and Mass Culture." *Social Text*, 1, pp. 130–148.

Jankélévitch, Vladimir. (1989 [1959]) *Henri Bergson*. Paris: Quadrige/PUF.

———. (1974) *L'irréversible et la nostalgie*. Paris: Flammarion.

Juteau, Danielle, and Nicole Laurin. (1989) "From Nuns to Surrogate Mothers: Evolution of the Forms of the Appropriation of Women." *Feminist Issues*, 9:1, pp. 13–40.

Kaplan, Caren. (1994) "The 'Good Neighbor' Policy Meets the 'Feminine Mystique': The Geopolitics of the Domestic Sitcom." Paper presented at the Society for Cinema Studies, Syracuse.

Kates, Nancy D. (1993) "My Mother's Worst Fears." In B. L. Singer (ed.), *Growing Up Gay*. New York: Free Press, pp. 126–32.

Kroker, Arthur. (1984) *Technology and the Canadian Mind: Innis/McLuhan/Grant*. Montréal: New World Perspectives.

Lynch, Lee. (1990) "Cruising the Libraries." In Karla Jay and Joanne Glasgow (eds.), *Lesbian Texts and Contexts*. New York: New York University Press.

Machery, Pierre. (1992) "Présentation: Foucault/Roussel/Foucault." *Raymond Roussel*. Paris: Seuil.

Marsan, Jean-Claude. (1994) *Montréal en évolution: Historique du développement de l'architecture et de l'environnement urbain montréalais*. Montréal: Méridien.

Martin, Biddy. (1994) "Sexualities Without Genders and Other Queer Utopias." *diacritics*, 24:2–3, pp. 104–121.

———. (1982/1988) "Feminism, Criticism, and Foucault." In Irene Diamond and Lee Quimby (eds.), *Feminism & Foucault: Reflections on Resistance*. Boston: Northwestern University Press.

Martin, Robert. (1994) "L'identité homosexuelle post-identitaire." Paper presented at Les cultures gaie et lesbienne, Université de Québec à Montréal.

Massumi, Brian. (1992) *A User's Guide to CAPITALISM AND SCHIZOPHRE-NIA*. Cambridge: The MIT Press.

Mathieu, Nicole-Claude. (1989) "Identité sexuelle/sexuée/de sexe? Trois modes de conceptualisation du rapport entre le sexe et le genre." In Anne-Marie Duane-Richard, Marie-Claude Hurtig and Marie-France Pichevin (eds.), *Catégorisations de sexe et constructions scientifiques*. Aix-en-Provence: CEFUP.

May, Todd G. (1991) "The Politics of Life in the Thought of Gilles Deleuze." *Substance*, 20:66, pp. 24–35.

Mayne, Judith. (1992) "*LA Law* and Prime Time Lesbianism." Paper presented at the Console-ing Passions Conference, University of Iowa.

———. (1991) "A Parallax View of Lesbian Authorship." In Diana Fuss (ed.), *Inside/out: Lesbian Theories, Gay Theories*. New York and London: Routledge.

Mbembe, Achille. "The Banality of Power and the Aesthetics of Vulgarity in the Postcolony." *Public Culture*, 4:2, pp. 1–30.

Ménard, Guy. (1983) *Une Rumeur de Berdaches: Contribution à une lecture de l'homosexualité masculine au Québec*. Unpublished doctoral thesis. Département des études réligieuses, Université de Paris 7.

Mitford, Nancy. (1949) *Love in a Cold Climate*. Middlesex: Penguin.

Monteagudo, Jesse G. (1992) "Miami, Florida." In J. Preston (ed.), *Hometowns: Gay Men Write About Where They Belong*. New York: Plume, pp. 11–20.

Moon, Michael. (1993) "New Introduction." In Guy Hocquenghem, *Homosexual Desire*. Translated by Daniella Dangoor. Durham: Duke University Press.

Morris, Meaghan. "A Gadfly Bites Back." *Meanjin*, 3, pp. 545–551.

Morton, Donald. (1993) "The Politics of Queer Theory in the (Post)Modern Moment." *Genders*, 17, pp. 121–147.

Muecke, Stephen. (1992) *Textual Spaces: Aboriginality and Cultural Studies*. Sydney: New South Wales University Press.

Nadeau, Chantal. (1993) *Discours de l'autre, représentation de l'altérité: Vers une position d'énonciation filmique féministe*. Unpublished Doctoral thesis. Département de sociologie, Université de Montréal.

————. (1992) "Women in French-Québec Cinema: The Space of Socio-Sexual Indifference." *Cinéaction*, 28, pp. 4–15.

Namaste, Ki. (1994a) "Tragic Misreadings: Queer Theory's Erasure of Transgender Subjectivity." Paper presented at The Sixth North American Lesbian, Gay, and Bisexual Studies Conference, University of Iowa.

————. (1994b) "The Politics of Inside/Out: Queer Theory, Poststructuralism, and a Sociological Approach to Sexuality." *Sociological Theory*, 12, pp. 220–231.

Nava, Michael. (1992) "Gardenland, Sacramento, California." In J. Preston (ed.), *Hometowns: Gay Men Write About Where They Belong*. New York: Plume, pp. 21–29.

Nietzsche, Friedrich. (1972 [1909–1911]) "On Truth and Falsity in Their Extramoral Sense." In Warren Shibles (ed.), *Essays on Metaphor*. Wisconsin: The Language Press.

Normand, Claudine. (1976) *Métaphore et concept*. Bruxelles: Édition Complexe.

Nothomb, Amélie. (1993) *Le sabotage amoureux*. Paris: Albin Michel.

Paris, Sherri. (1993) "Review of *A Lure for Knowledge: Lesbian Sexuality and Theory* by Judith Roof and *Inside/out: Lesbian Theories, Gay Theories* edited by Diana Fuss." *Signs*, 18:4, pp. 984–988.

Parker, Andrew. (1993) "Unthinking Sex: Marx, Engels, and the Scene of Writing." In Michael Warner (ed.), *Fear of a Queer Planet: Queer Politics and Social Theory*. Minneapolis: University of Minnesota Press.

————, Mary Russo, Doris Sommer, and Patricia Yeager (eds.). (1992) *Nationalisms and Sexualities*. New York and London: Routledge.

Patton, Cindy. (1993) "Tremble, Hetero Swine!" In Michael Warner (ed.), *Fear of a Queer Planet: Queer Politics and Social Theory*. Minneapolis: University of Minnesota Press.

Patton, Paul. (1995) "Society as Virtual Idea and as Event." Paper presented at the International Association of Philosophy and Literature.

Paul, Jay J. (1993) "Childhood Cross-Gender Behavior and Adult Homosexuality: The Resurgence of Biological Models of Sexuality." *Journal of Homosexuality*, 24, pp. 41–54.

Peck, Dale. (1993) *Martin and John*. New York: HarperPerennial.

Phillips, Gabriel, M. Psych, and Ray Over. (1992) "Adult Sexual Orientation in Relation to Memories of Childhood Gender Conforming and Gender Nonconforming Behaviors." *Archives of Sexual Behavior*, 21, pp. 543–558.

Philo, C. (1992) "Foucault's Geography." *Environment and Planning D: Society and Space*, 10, pp. 137–161.

Preston, John (ed.). (1992) *Hometowns: Gay Men Write About Where They Belong*. New York: Plume.

Probyn, Elspeth. (forthcoming) *Governing by Choice: Feminism, Desire and Subjectification*. Minneapolis: University of Minnesota Press.

————. (1995) "Lesbians in Space: Gender, Sex and the Structure of Missing." *Gender, Place and Culture*, 2:1, pp. 77–84.

————. (1993) *Sexing the Self: Gendered Positions in Cultural Studies*. London and New York: Routledge.

————, (ed.). (1992) *Entre le corps et le soi: Une sociologie de la subjectivation*. *Sociologie et sociétés*, 24:1. Montréal: Les Presses de l'Université de Montréal.

Pronger, Brian. (1993) "On Your Knees: Getting Down to the Queer." Paper presented at the Queer Sites Conference, University of Toronto.

Radford, Jean. (1986) "An Inverted Romance: *The Well of Loneliness* and Sexual Ideology." In Jean Radford (ed.), *The Progress of Romance: The Politics of Popular Fiction*. London: Routledge & Kegan Paul.

Reynolds, Margaret. (1993) "Introduction." In M. Reynolds (ed.), *The Penguin Book of Lesbian Short Stories*. London: Penguin, pp. xiii–xxxiii.

Rich, Adrienne. (1986) *Blood, Bread and Poetry*. New York: W.W. Norton.

Robson, Ruthann. (1992) "Sabrina's Horses." *Common Lives/Lesbian Lives*, 42, pp. 109–114.

Ropars-Wuilleumier, Marie-Claire. (1988) "The Cinema, Reader of Gilles Deleuze." *Camera Obscura*, 18, pp. 120–126.

Rose, Nikolas, and Peter Miller. (1992) "Political Power Beyond the State: Problematics of Government." *British Journal of Sociology*, 23:2, pp. 173–205.

Roussel, Raymond. (1963) *Comment j'ai écrit certains de mes livres*. Paris: J-J Pauvert.

Saint-Jacques, Denis, and Roger de la Garde. (1992) "Une culture pour l'Amérique francophone d'aujourd'hui et de demain: Arlette Cousture, Roch Voisine, CROC et Bernard Derome." In Denis Saint-Jacques, Roger de la Garde (eds.), *Les pratiques culturelles de grande consommation*. Québec: Nuit Blanche Editeur.

Saslow, James M. (1992) "'Disagreeably Hidden': Construction of the Lesbian Body in Rosa Bonheur's *Horse Fair*." In Norma Broude and Mary Garrard (eds.), *The Expanding Discourse: Feminism and Art History*. New York: HarperCollins.

Savoy, Eric. (1995) "The Signifying Rabbit." *Narratives*, 3:2, pp. 188–209.

———. (1994) "You Can't Go Homo Again: Queer Theory and the Foreclosure of Gay Studies." *English Studies in Canada*, 20, pp. 129–152.

Sawhney, Sabina. (1995) "The Jewels in the Crotch: The Imperial Erotic in *The Raj Quartet*." In Elizabeth Grosz and Elspeth Probyn (eds.), *Sexy Bodies: The Strange Carnalities of Feminism*. London and New York: Routledge.

Saylor, Steven. (1993) "A World of Possibilities." In B. L. Singer (ed.), *Growing Up Gay*. New York: Free Press, pp. 52–53.

Schwarztwald, Robert. (1993) "'Symbolic' Homosexuality, 'False Feminine', and the Problematics of Identity in Québec." In Michael Warner (ed.), *Fear of a Queer Planet: Queer Politics and Social Theory*. Minneapolis: University of Minnesota Press.

———. (1991) "Fear of Federasty: Québec's Inverted Fictions." In Hortense J. Spillers (ed.), *Comparative American Identities: Race, Sex and Nationality in the Modern Text*. New York and London: Routledge.

Sedgwick, Eve Kosofsky. (1993) *Tendencies*. Durham: Duke University Press.

———. (1990) *Epistemology of the Closet*. Berkeley: University of California Press.

———. (1985) *Between Men: English Literature and Male Homosocial Desire*. New York: Columbia University Press.

Simon, Sherry. (1991) "Notes from la rue Jeanne-Mance." *Matrix*, 35, pp. 21–23.

Singer, Bennett L. (ed.). (1993) *Growing Up Gay*. New York: Free Press.

Soja, Edward W. (1995) "Heterotopologies: A Remembrance of Other Spaces in the Citadel-LA." In Sophie Watson and Katherine Gibson (eds.), *Postmodern Cities and Spaces*. Oxford: Blackwell.

Spark, Muriel. (1961) *The Prime of Miss Jean Brodie*. Harmondsworth: Penguin.

Spigel, Lynn. (1988) "Installing the Television Set: Popular Discourses on Television and Domestic Space." *Camera Obscura*, 16, pp. 11–46.

Starobinski, Jean. (1966) "Le concept de nostalgie." *Diogène*, 54, pp. 92–115.

Stone, Sandy. (1992) "The Empire Strikes Back: A Posttranssexual Manifesto." *Camera Obscura*, 29, pp. 151–176.

Straw, Will. (1992) "Montréal Confidential: Notes on an Imagined City." *Cinéaction*, 28, pp. 58–65.

Tremblay, Michel. (1993) *Le coeur éclaté*. Montréal: Lémeac.

———. (1990) *La maison suspendue*. Montréal: Lémeac.

Vallières, Pierre. (1968) *Négres blancs d'Amérique*. Montréal: Partis Pris.

Vattimo, Gianni. (1987) *La fin de la modernité: Nihilism and herméneutique dans la culture post-moderne*. Paris: Seuil.

Watney, Simon. (1993) "AIDS and the Politics of Queer Diaspora." Public Lecture, L'Université de Montréal.

Waugh, Thomas. (1980) "Nègres blancs, tapettes et 'butch': Les lesbiennes et les gais dans le cinéma québécois." *Copie Zéro*, 11, pp. 12–29.

Weeks, Jeffrey. (1993) "Preface to the 1978 Edition." In Guy Hocquenghem, *Homosexual Desire*. Translated by Daniella Dangoor. Durham: Duke University Press.

White, Edmund. (1982) *A Boy's Own Story*. New York: Plume.

Whitlock, Gillian. (1987) "'Everything Is Out of Place': Radclyffe Hall and the Lesbian Literary Tradition." *Feminist Studies*, 13:3, pp. 555–582.

Wiegman, Robyn. (1994) "Introduction: Mapping the Lesbian Postmodern." In Laura Doan (ed.), *The Lesbian Postmodern*. New York: Columbia University Press.

Williams, Raymond. (1989) "The Future of Cultural Studies." *The Politics of Modernism*. London: Verso.

———. (1979) *Politics and Letters*. London: Verso.

———. (1976) *Keywords*. London: Fontana.

Winterson, Jeanette. (1991 [1985]) *Oranges Are Not the Only Fruit*. London: Bloomsbury Classics.

Wittig, Monique. (1992) *The Straight Mind*. Boston: Beacon Press.

index

A Lure for Knowledge, 138

Agamben, Giorgio, 21, 22, 24, 25, 27, 44, 68, 101

AIDS, 97, 138, 146

Allison, Dorothy, 31

Althusser, Louis, 25, 139, 145

amorous melancholia, 114

Anne of Green Gables, 82, 104

Anthropologie in pragmatischer Hinsichtabgefasst, 115

Anshaw, Carol, 41

Anzaldùa, Gloria, 31

Appadurai, Arjun, 147

Aquin, Hubert, 77, 78

Arcand, Denys, 86, 87

architecture 3, 146

Baudrillard, Jean, 34

becoming, 6, 7, 88–90, 103, 118, 119, 121, 144; becoming–other, 5, 14, 15, 76, 138, 153; becoming–horse, 39–62; becoming–postcolonial, 19, 27; becoming–queer, 19, 137

Bell, David, 10

Bellour, Raymond, 45, 55, 102

Benjamin, Walter, 19

Bergson, Henri, 53, 61, 117, 118

Berlant, Lauren, 145

Berthelot, Jean Michel, 72

Bhabha, Homi, 19–21, 26–28, 30, 34

Billingham, R.E., 105

Boyd, Marian, 104

Braidotti, Rosi, 41, 47, 110

Brault, Michel, 65, 80, 89

Brossard, Nicole, 59, 60

Brunt, Rosalind, 143

Butler, Judith, 13, 14, 25, 47, 56

childhood, 35, 95–101, 103–119, 121–123

chronotype, 35

Cixous, Hélène, 53

Colette, 56–58, 78

communication, 41–44, 74, 145

cooption, 141, 144, 146, 150

Cosmic Zoom, 73

Crimp, Douglas, 138

cultural criticism, 12, 41, 46, 52

cultural insider, 135, 144, 151

cultural studies, 5, 19, 22, 34, 95, 127, 129–132, 135, 138–142, 144, 148, 151

de Lauretis, Teresa, 47, 78, 138–140

Deleuze, Gilles, 7, 13–15, 24, 25, 41, 44, 45, 47–55, 61, 69, 71, 76, 91, 95, 117, 118, 133, 134, 148, 149, 153

Delphy, Christine, 78

departure, 13, 31, 45, 47, 66, 96, 98, 99, 123, 130, 136

depth, 32, 34, 35, 71, 121, 136

desire, 32–35, 39–50, 71, 88–90, 109, 110, 115, 116, 152; and belonging, 8, 14, 19, 23, 27, 35, 40, 89; as force, 27–30; productive, 12–14; and psychoanalysis, 46; lesbian, 13, 20, 25, 95; queer, 25, 46, 53, 61

Donzelot, Jacques, 134, 147

Doty, Alexander, 138, 144, 151

Dyer, Richard, 9

Enfance et histoire, 101

ethnicity, 5, 59, 62, 77, 79, 106, 127

feminism, 46, 69, 78, 79, 95, 129, 130, 135, 141

Fennario, David, 3

Foucault, Michel, 7, 9–14, 23–25, 29, 31–34, 43, 47, 48, 52, 53, 61, 95–97, 101, 102, 112, 113, 132, 133, 142, 145, 148, 149, 153

Frémont, Christiane, 69

Freud, Sigmund, 35, 50, 102

Fuss, Diana, 47, 137, 138

Galford, Ellen, 20, 21

Gatens, Moira, 41

gaze, 30, 53, 117

gender, 5, 10, 23, 35, 56, 57, 62, 67, 68, 72, 78, 79, 85, 89, 90, 96, 100, 105–110, 117, 139, 144, 152

genealogy, 96, 112, 113, 116, 139

Gilroy, Paul, 135–137

global, the, 69, 137, 140, 146, 147

Gomez, Jewelle, 23, 30, 31

Gordon, Colin, 14, 59, 75, 132

Gramsci, Antonio, 143, 145

Grossberg, Lawrence, 34, 43, 44

Grosz, Elizabeth, 13, 41, 46, 47, 49, 51, 52, 55, 59, 133, 151, 153

Grover, Jan Zita, 138

Guattari, Felix, 24, 43, 44, 49–51, 54, 149

Guillaumin, Colette, 78, 79, 139

Hall, Radclyffe, 58

Hall, Stuart, 5, 6, 25, 145, 149

Halperin, David, 11, 47, 48

Haraway, Donna, 6

Heal, Linda, 109

Hennegan, Alison, 58

Hennessy, Rosemary, 139–141, 143

heterosexual, 57, 79, 81, 86–88, 103, 106, 107

heterotopia, 9–11

HIV, 146

Hockenberry, S.L., 105

Hoggart, Richard, 141

Hometowns: Gay Men Write About Where They Belong, 110

homosexuality, 28, 31, 35, 86–88, 106–108

homosociality, 78, 79, 81, 82, 86, 90, 106

horses, 11, 30, 39, 41, 45, 50–52, 54–60, 62, 82–84

Hutcheon, Linda, 74, 77

identity, 3–5, 8, 21–25, 28–30, 47, 54, 81–84, 95, 96, 99, 100, 108, 110, 113, 136, 137, 139, 141, 143, 146, 151, 152; childhood, 96, 99, 105; identity politics, 9, 14, 19, 41, 44, 96; Québécois, 67–78, 84, 86–90

Innis, Harold, 74, 75

Inside/Out, 137

interiority, 11, 12, 35, 148

Jackson, Michael, 65, 89
Jameson, Fredric, 77, 78
Jankélévitch, Vladimir, 114, 116, 117
Julien, Isaac, 31

Kant, Immanuel, 115
Kaplan, Cora, 145
Kates, Nancy, 108
KKK, 65, 89

La maison suspendue, 119, 120
Lacan, Jacques, 46
language, 4, 6, 8, 12, 14, 21, 24–26, 31,
    33, 35, 44, 58, 72, 101, 102, 127, 129,
    145, 149–151
Le Déclin de l'empire américain, 86
Le sabotage amoureux, 95
Lefebvre, Jean–Pierre, 73
Les Filles de Caleb, 81–85, 150
Lightfoot, Gordon, 75
lips, 56, 66, 78, 89
local, the, 30, 52, 69, 71, 110, 111, 115,
    129, 131, 132, 134, 137, 140, 142, 146,
    147, 149
locomotion, 11, 41
Logique du sens, 96
Love in a Cold Climate, 27, 28, 65

Machery, Pierre, 31–33
Making Things Perfectly Queer, 144
Mandel, Eli, 74
marginalization, 11, 29, 48, 72–75, 84,
    141
Marnie, 45, 46, 55
Marsan, Jean–Claude, 3
Martin, Biddy, 12, 46, 73, 97

Masala, 40
Massumi, Brian, 24, 48, 53
materiality, 6, 10, 12, 24, 69, 76, 78, 79,
    83, 110, 131, 136, 137, 141
Mathieu, Nicole–Claude, 78, 119, 120
Mbembe, Achille, 29, 30
McLuhan, Marshall, 74
memory, 20, 21, 40, 41, 57, 81, 84,
    96–102, 103–107, 109–118, 120–122,
    136
Miller, Peter, 130, 145–148, 151
Mitford, Nancy, 27, 28
Moderato Cantabile, 53
Montréal, 3–5, 8, 25–27, 30, 65, 66, 69,
    70, 74, 80, 85–87, 91, 104, 119, 120,
    127, 128, 153
Montréal ville ouverte, 85
Montréal, P.Q., 85
Morris, Meaghan, 135
Morton, Donald, 139, 141–144
Muecke, Stephen, 72
My Brilliant Career, 82
My Friend Flicka, 54

National Velvet, 54
Negri, Toni, 148
Nestle, Joan, 31
Nietzsche, Friedrich, 43, 97, 113
Northern Exposure, 76, 77
nostalgia, 35, 91, 95, 103, 111, 112,
    114–118, 121, 122
Nothomb, Amélie 95

Oranges Are Not the Only Fruit, 111, 112
outside belonging, 5, 8, 12, 14
Paris, Sherri, 138, 139

Parler pour Parler, 87

Patton, Paul, 50, 148, 151

Paul, Jay, 105

Peck, Dale, 97

phallus, 46, 58, 59

Philo, Chris, 33, 34

Plain and Tall, 82

pleasure, 45, 47, 48, 58, 84, 139, 142, 144

postmodernism, 8, 77, 129, 142

power, 28–30, 45, 47, 48, 51, 57, 72–74, 86, 133, 134, 142, 145, 146, 149, 151

psychiatry, 99, 108

psychoanalysis, 46, 47, 50, 99, 108, 116

Québec, 5, 26, 30, 65–67, 71–74, 78, 80, 81, 84, 86–90, 103, 104, 119, 127, 150

queer theory, 12, 13, 69, 96, 101, 129, 138–142, 146

racism, 6, 32, 139

Radford, Jean, 58

Railroad Trilogy, 75

Raymond Roussel, 31, 33

Revel, Jacques, 102

Reynolds, Margaret, 111

Robson, Ruthann, 59

Roof, Judith, 138

Rose, Nikolas, 130, 145–148, 151

s/m, 48, 86, 87

Said, Edward, 20

Sarah, 82

Savoy, Eric, 55, 137–139

Sawhney, Sabina, 27

Sedgwick, Eve Kosofsky, 13, 14, 25,

100, 101, 105

Segrest, Mab, 31

Sexing the Self, 6

sexuality, 20, 32, 48, 67, 78, 79, 84, 89, 90, 105, 129, 130, 132, 136, 141, 145, 150–152; childhood, 99, 108, 109, 116; and difference, 23, 59, 68, 71, 72; queer, 28, 189; Havelock Ellis, 58

Simon, Sherry, 3, 4

singularity, 3, 4, 9, 10, 13, 15, 21–24, 27, 31, 41, 42, 51, 53, 58, 68, 69, 71, 72, 76, 78, 84, 89, 90, 97, 110, 111, 131, 132, 136, 152

skin, 5, 6, 14, 15, 128, 153

sociology of the skin, 5

Soja, Edward, 10

specificity, 9, 10, 22–24, 34, 42, 72, 136, 152

Starobinski, Jean, 114, 115

stigmata, 101

surface, 11–15, 19–21, 23, 28–35, 45, 53, 71, 77, 78, 96, 101–103, 107, 121, 122, 130, 131, 136–139, 141, 144, 145, 148, 150–153

technology of the self, 102

The Dyke and the Dybbuk, 20

The King and I, 82

The Lesbian Postmodern, 138

The Order of Things, 7

The Prime of Miss Jean Brodie, 82

The Pure and the Impure, 56

The Simpsons, 145

The Straight Mind, 139

The Well of Loneliness, 57, 58

trains, 8, 11, 39, 40, 75
translation, 20, 26, 31, 53, 147–149, 151
transportation, 41
Tremblay, Michel, 66, 86, 87, 119, 121

Vattimo, Gianno, 134
Vigneault, Gilles, 74, 80
Volatile Bodies, 49
Voltaire, François, 74

White, Edmund, 99,
White, Hayden, 11,
Wiegman, Robyn, 138
Williams, Raymond, 131, 132, 141
Winterson, Jeanette, 111–113, 120
Wittig, Monique, 139

Ybarra-Frausto, Tomas, 30, 31